THE
UNGARNISHED
TRUTH

THE
UNGARNISHED
TRUTH

A Cooking Contest Memoir

ELLIE MATHEWS

BERKLEY BOOKS, NEW YORK

THE BERKLEY PUBLISHING GROUP
Published by the Penguin Group
Penguin Group (USA) Inc.
375 Hudson Street, New York, New York 10014, USA

Penguin Group (Canada), 90 Englinton Avenue East, Suite 700, Toronto, Ontario M4P 2Y3 Canada (a division of Pearson Penguin Canada Inc.)
Penguin Books Ltd., 80 Strand, London WC2R 0RL, England
Penguin Group Ireland, 25 St. Stephen's Green, Dublin 2, Ireland (a division of Penguin Books Ltd.)
Penguin Group (Australia), 250 Camberwell Road, Camberwell, Victoria 3124, Australia (a division of Pearson Australia Group Pty. Ltd.)
Penguin Books India Pvt. Ltd., 11 Community Centre, Panchsheel Park, New Delhi—110 017, India
Penguin Group (NZ), 67 Apollo Drive, Rosedale, North Shore 0632, New Zealand (a division of Pearson New Zealand Ltd.)
Penguin Books (South Africa) (Pty.) Ltd., 24 Sturdee Avenue, Rosebank, Johannesburg 2196, South Africa

Penguin Books Ltd., Registered Offices: 80 Strand, London, WC2R, 0RL England

This book is an original publication of The Berkley Publishing Group.

Bake-Off and other trademarks are the property of General Mills, used with permission. All other trademarks are the property of their respective owners.

This book is not affiliated with or endorsed by General Mills. While General Mills was consulted regarding certain facts, the information and opinions contained in this book are those of the author and do not represent the opinion of General Mills.

The recipe contained in this book is to be followed exactly as written. The publisher is not responsible for your specific health or allergy needs that may require medical supervision. The publisher is not responsible for any adverse reactions to the recipe contained in this book. The publisher does not have any control over and does assume any responsibility for author or third-party websites or their content.

First edition : March 2008

Library of Congress Cataloging-in-Publication Data

Mathews, Ellie.
   The ungarnished truth : a cooking contest memoir / Ellie Mathews.
      p. cm.
   ISBN-13: 978-0-425-21945-4
   1. Mathews, Ellie. 2. Cooks—Biography. I. Title.
TX649.M36 2007
641. 5092—dc22
[B]
                              2007018722

PRINTED IN THE UNITED STATES OF AMERICA

10 9 8 7 6 5 4 3 2 1

*For
Karen,
Carl & Loa
in order
of appearance
at the table*

ACKNOWLEDGMENTS

May the teamwork that went into this book stand as evidence that a multiplicity of cooks doesn't necessarily spoil the broth. Janet Cox, Ruth Whitney, Pat Simpson, Sheila Bender, Bob Kaye, and Jason Sciarrone egged me on from start to finish. They kept the pot from boiling over while helping me season the manuscript and temper the story. I thank them for all that and more. For a peppering of corrections, advice, and assistance, I thank Tom Aslin, Kit Bakke, Lisa Keys, Norita Solt, Mary DeFelice-Bartley, and the people at Pillsbury. I thank my agent, Elizabeth Wales, for pairing me with Jackie Cantor and Berkley Books. And I thank Jackie for guiding me through the editing process with wisdom, patience, and humor. From this author's perspective, it was a match made in heaven.

For everything else, I thank Carl Youngmann. About him I could go on and on (and often do).

CHAPTER ONE

I was up a ladder when the call came about appearing on the Oprah show. You might think that a woman in her fifties would hire an expert, but even after I'd won the Pillsbury Bake-Off, I was still obsessed with the idea of self-reliance and self-sufficiency. Maybe that fixation had been a factor when it came to entering the contest in the first place. My husband, Carl, had answered the call in his office on the third floor of our historic, and slightly creaky, Seattle house. He handed the phone up to me on the ladder, where I was experimenting with real plaster for the first time. The stuff was setting up fast and I was aware of being slow at smearing it on. Our kitchen ceiling was cracked right down to the lath.

"They want you to do the Oprah show," Carl said.

I muffled the phone against my sweatshirt with one hand, whispered, "This is Oprah *Winfrey*?" while extracting a plaster glob from my hair with my other. Hardly the glamour image of television appearances.

"No, no. It's Marlene Johnson," Carl said.

I let out the breath I'd been unconsciously holding. Marlene was the Pillsbury public relations director who had eased me through other television appearances a year before. I would have jumped on just about any plane she wanted me to board and faced any camera she wanted me to smile toward. After all, she and her company had awarded me a million bucks for cooking eight chicken thighs in their brand of salsa.

Not that I'm a media hound. Far from it. Some people will do all kinds of crazy things to get themselves on television. My allegiance to Marlene Johnson and company was another matter altogether. Two days later I was on a plane bound for Chicago, for the purpose of holding up a jar of Old El Paso Salsa on national television for a total of one second. It would turn out to be my last act as the reigning queen of chickendom.

I didn't have to worry about what clothes to pack. Right after the Bake-Off, Pillsbury had outfitted me with an inoffensive, all-purpose ensemble in colors guaranteed not to smear, crawl, or bleed on television. Shoes, belt, socks, the works. And nothing from the markdown rack, either. The turtleneck and khakis fulfilled the PR department's vision of what an all-American, clean-cut cook should look like. Knowing it served their purposes gave me comfort. I wanted to perform well for Pillsbury. I liked Pillsbury.

At O'Hare Airport a woman held a card bearing my name to fish me out of the ocean of travelers. As a limousine driver, she picked up guests not only for the Oprah show but for the Jerry Springer and Jenny Jones shows. I perched on the edge of white leather in the back, acres away from the driver's seat. We had to shout over the distance. She eased into traffic and, by way of making conversation, volunteered she could tell immediately which of the three hosts I was scheduled with. I guess I didn't look the type to have castrated my neighbors' Airedale with a can opener or to have had sex with a bull moose while riding a bicycle through Central Park.

Pillsbury had paid eighteen hundred bucks for my short-notice airplane ticket, and that didn't even seat me in first class. I obsessed with some rough arithmetic as we nosed toward downtown Chicago: if a jar of salsa retails for x and the retailer marks it up by y...and the jar itself costs something, and the lid, and the label, and a machine to glue it on with...and the product inside...then how many additional units would Pillsbury have to sell to recover the cost of me making this trip? I felt the weight of responsibility—me, the Salsa Ambassador.

In Chicago, the show put me up. As is stated in the closing credits, guests of *The Oprah Winfrey Show* stay at Chicago's Omni Hotel. At the registration desk I was handed chits for dinner and breakfast in the amounts of fifty and twenty-five dollars. I didn't think for a minute I'd be able to spend that much on two simple meals, more than my monthly grocery budget the first year I was married.

The producer for the show called that evening to go over what to expect the next morning, when another white limousine would pick me up and take me to the Harpo Studios. I was to be one of many guests on that day's episode. The theme was contest winners. I wouldn't be sitting thigh-to-thigh with Oprah herself. Rather, I'd be placed in the audience with other guests to be called upon one by one. I was okay with that. What I didn't know to anticipate was that the audience would be directed to exhibit a frenzy of squeals and adoration the minute Oprah popped onto the set. By sitting with her fans, I'd either have to follow along or look like a sourpuss. But I'm not a natural-born squealer in situations like that. This personality quirk had been a problem ever since winning the million.

THE first recipe contest I entered was hugely small-time. Recreational Equipment Company (REI), which still felt like the co-op it advertises itself to be, set up half a dozen backpacker's stoves on folding tables in the basement of its then main store on Capitol Hill in my Seattle neighborhood. The idea was to see who could combine little packets of freeze-dried food into the best simulation of a meal anyone would want to gag down on a camping trip.

This was 1980, a time when my family were avid backpackers, with summer weekends finding us on one Cascade Mountain trail or another. Food for those trips was almost a competition in itself as we coordinated with hiking companions on communal meals. It was all about balancing the equations of ingredients that would keep without refrigeration, didn't weigh more than a few ounces, would cook quickly over our little gas stove (about the size of a tuna fish can), and wouldn't require elaborate cleanup or generate complicated garbage to pack out. On top of all that we wanted meals that would taste good and restore our spirits after a tough day on the trail.

My biggest successes often involved bulgur wheat, for its whole-grain integrity, its ability to cook almost instantly without excess boiled water to dispose of onto the wilderness, and its natural adaptation to an assortment of seasonings. Carl and I devised a recipe for a one-pot meal of potato flakes, too, fortified with powdered milk and powdered egg, then added dried onion and chipped beef. Put yourself in the high country and anything can become a feast. I loved the puzzle of balancing fuel efficiency with cost and effort and the number of calories required to make it safely back to home ground. If the results could taste good, too, so much the better.

On those trips I would sometimes fall asleep under the stars while devising menu possibilities for our next wilderness assault. Solving a puzzle while drifting off is my idea of relaxation. With the intensity of NASA precision, I'd calculate how much Tang to repackage into Ziplocs for five people on a three-day trip, or what could be done to replace the MSG packets that come with instant ramen. Give me a problem to solve—whether it's a Sunday crossword or a brain teaser—and I'm like a dog with a bone. So when REI came along with their contest, it felt natural to enter. I had already considered the problem of backpacker recipes in some depth.

The event was pleasantly thrown together. Not many participants showed up. Maybe others were out on the trail on that sunny summer Saturday. My mother, tall and capable, my daughter, and I all entered, and, as it turned out, each of us placed. At the store we cooked in little aluminum pots as if we were really on a trek of some sort, although we didn't cook on the floor in simulation of the inconveniences of real camping. My mother made spaghetti dressed in something akin to desiccated pesto; I made whole-grain pancakes using instant brown rice. My daughter, Karen, a willowy fifteen-year-old at the time, had stumbled against our kitchen door in the rush to get to the store on time. I don't know whether the resulting black eye elicited the judges' sympathy or what, but they awarded her first place for her freeze-dried chili with dumplings made from a Jiffy corn muffin mix, powdered milk, and powdered eggs. Hardly haute cuisine, but compromises must be made when it comes to lightweight camping.

A few years later, Carl and I picked up a page of recipes in the cattle barn at the Western Washington State Fair. On it was a call for entries in the state Beef Cook-Off. First place was worth $300 and the possibility of going to the national cook-off where someone would walk away with a whopping $15,000. Well, okay, I thought. I remember having the sense that we ate pretty well most nights at our house. Maybe I had something to offer. This beef contest seemed like something that might be worth a try.

We were eating beef once or twice a week back then. I wanted to see whether anyone would think I measured up if I told them how I made dinner.

Lacking the belief that anything serious would come of it, I didn't fret over refining a recipe. Using the basic components of Russian borscht but without chopping and dicing as if for soup, I made a pot roast one evening with beets, carrots, potatoes, and cabbage. This I seasoned with a splash of cider vinegar, a can of tomatoes, plenty of dried dill weed, and a big fat onion. After the simmering, I stirred a cup of sour cream into the resulting liquid and arranged everything on a platter: Siberian Beef. It tasted pretty good. I mailed in the recipe.

Some weeks later a packet of information arrived from the Beef Commission inviting me to participate with nine other people as finalists at the cook-off.

My confession is that I didn't take any of it very seriously. For one thing, it had been too easy. Therefore, I assumed the selection process wasn't a rigorous one. Also, the finals were to be held in Kennewick, on the other side of the state and not exactly a tourist hot spot. I'd have to haul myself over there at my own expense. And, frankly, it sounded a little bit hokey. Red bandanas and all.

At the last minute I decided not to be a stick-in-the-mud. I took a deep breath and lightened up. Carl and I made arrangements to go. I'm glad we did. He didn't have to come with me, but we do almost everything together when humanly possible. Most of our outings to the grocery store, for example, are a twosome. We sometimes read the paper side by side, turning the page only when we're both ready. We fold the laundry together; he takes the towels and sheets while I match the socks. Carl and I are not only joined at the hip, we've got our shoulders and ankles linked as well.

The event was sponsored by the Washington CowBelles Association. Yes, that really was their name. They've since changed it to Cattlewomen, having evolved from the concept of a ranchers' wives club to an agricultural force all their own. The Beef Commission is a state agency funded by a one-dollar assessment on each head of cattle sold in the state. An additional fifty cents per beast is collected for product promotion. That's where the contest came in.

With a sense of adventure, Carl and I set off for the wilds of central Washington. Given that I'd likely be going home empty-handed and not wanting to go into the hole on this gamble, we kept a tight hold on our wallet and found a place to camp between the Columbia River and a ripening asparagus field. The next morning, bright with spring's promise, we found our way to the lobby of Cavanaugh's Motor Inn and registered me for the contest.

Ten full-sized stoves had been set up in the main function room of the motel. Each finalist was given a red apron with the cook-off logo splashed across the front and each of us was assigned a similarly aproned volunteer CowBelle as helper and monitor, although those women weren't allowed to do any of the cooking. Not even tasting, suggesting, or commenting on methods.

Any thoughts I might have had that the experience would be too cornball for my smarty-pants, city attitude evaporated at the door. The CowBelles had clearly put their hearts and souls into making us feel welcome and comfortable. These women were salt-of-the-earth, good-natured, generous, and sincere. I immediately wanted them all to be my mother.

Finalists supplied their own ingredients and equipment. We had all morning to prepare our recipes. In the slack time while things marinated, simmered, sizzled, and broiled, we got to know each other—the cooks and the CowBelles. A few of the finalists were contest veterans. Someone mentioned having been to a national cook-off. Another turned me on to the existence of the *Cooking Contest Newsletter*. A nurse from Puyallup said she'd been to "Hunts," meaning the spaghetti sauce contest sponsored by the tomato company. A woman from the foothills of Mount Rainier owned a collection of several hundred cookbooks. Somebody knew somebody who had been to "the Pillsbury," as she put it. "At the Pillsbury they treat you like a queen," she said, "a real queen."

I wouldn't say I plunged headfirst into the world of cooking competitions that day, but I put a toe in the water all the way up to my instep. More for the curiosity than the hope of winning anything, I kept my radar tuned to the details of other contests as conversations floated by. I especially liked the notion of submitting entries by mail. I loved the idea of being nothing more than a random name—or better yet, a number—to contest sponsors. If I entered and my recipes got tossed into the shredder on the first cut, I wouldn't even have to be embarrassed. You can't beat anonymity when it comes to failing at something.

Meanwhile, there was my Siberian Beef bubbling away. Each of us had an assigned time to submit our dish to the judges, sequestered in another part of the building. They didn't know who we were and we wouldn't see them until after the prizes had been awarded.

Having prepared dinner almost every night of my adult life, I was not nervous at the prospect of cooking a pot roast. But my CowBelle was. Dolores had never monitored a cook-off. Rules were that she had to make sure I didn't slip anything extraneous into the pot. Once submitted, changes could not be made to the recipes. No problem. I had no intention of altering anything. She was also there to help me get the food onto a cart that would be used to wheel the stuff in to the judges, although she wasn't allowed to give advice or react to how I arranged things for presentation. Parsley/no parsley. Sauce on the side/sauce poured over the top.

Pot roast is the easiest thing in the world to make. Unless it involves adding sour cream at the last minute. Any good cook knows not to let it boil, or the cream will curdle. I should have taken my Dutch oven off the burner and set it aside for a minute or two. But I was careless. The instant I added the cream, I knew I'd made a mistake. The curdling process began on one side, and, as with a chemical reaction, the whole mass separated into something grainy and wrong looking. Too late to salvage the situation, I couldn't hide myself or my beef under a cabbage leaf, although I would have liked to. All I could do was submit the dish as I'd made it. I was disappointed with myself but not devastated. I'd gone there on a lark and I was having fun anyway. I hadn't imagined winning.

The afternoon was set aside for entertainment. And what did the beef producers think would be memorable? A trip to the feed lot. I had never thought about how interesting that would be, but where else would I ever get an up-close view of thousands of animals standing on a mountain of their own intestinal making while our guide gave details of the industry? How much the animals weighed. How much they gained. How long it took. How much it cost. What they ate. Among other things, the animals were fed a slurry of potato scraps, which were generated across the way at the French fry processing plant. It made for a genuine meat-and-potatoes lesson in agriculture. Carl's big brown eyes were wide. He kept nudging me and whispering things like "We couldn't *buy* an experience like this."

For a couple of city-dwelling software developers out of academia (Carl) and graphic design (me), a whole new world opened up. For dinner we were bused to the rolling green lawn of a five-star ranch house. Tables were set up on the grass overlooking the Columbia River. At five o'clock a man in cowboy boots and a string tie delivered a Christian blessing. The menu was...beef! my first exposure to a fajita, which I felt was a dandy invention.

After dinner a rancher representing the Beef Commission stepped forward to introduce the contest judges. One was the food editor of the *Wenatchee World*, a daily newspaper from the center of the state. Another was an employee of Haggen Foods, an upscale supermarket in Bellingham, near the Canadian border.

The rancher began with honorable mentions. I didn't get one. Then he announced third place. Not me. But that was okay. I hadn't expected to win. So when my name was called for second place, the announcer caught me off guard.

I learned later from the judges that had my sour cream not curdled I'd have been given first-place honors, which would have included an expense-paid trip to the national cook-off in Sun Valley, Idaho, and an opportunity to hobnob with James Garner, the celebrity du jour hired for the occasion. The funny thing about the judges' comments was this: they loved my vegetables, impressed that I'd used fresh beets. Cooking a beet is not exactly rocket surgery and steamed cabbage used to be everybody's bad joke in the vegetable world. I was surprised the judges hadn't focused primarily on the beef I'd sliced onto my platter. The cattle industry was sponsoring this shindig. I was impressed the beef people weren't fixated on their own product and that they'd given the judges plenty of latitude to consider the entire dish. I liked being among people who understood food in some of the same ways I did.

Coming that close to winning first place was enough encouragement to motivate me to enter again the following year and the year after that and the year after that. By then Carl had rolled up his sleeves in the kitchen and joined in the fun. We were both eligible to enter. And wouldn't you know, he came in first in our state competition the following year with something he called

French Beef with Filbert Barley. Again, it was a pot roast, the specialty of our house, I guess, since we generally shop low on the hog. Or the steer. He seasoned it with mustard, tarragon, and a whiff of fresh tomato. He hoped the novelty of barley would catch the judges' attention. Apparently it did.

A few months later, we flew to Jackson, Mississippi, Carl's expenses covered by the industry. I used a mileage award. At the hotel we met forty-nine other hopeful cooks, one from each state. It was my first peek at the inner workings of a national cook-off.

Neither of us had ever been in the Deep South. Carl and I had both earned degrees in geography. We're interested in terrain and what it supports and how people adapt to living on it. We lapped up the details of this new landscape and its cultural influences, starting with its cuisine. We ate boiled peanuts. Hush puppies. Catfish. One evening there was a trip to a farm museum. The next afternoon we were bused to a white-pillared mansion where women dressed in antebellum gowns over hoop skirts served us triangular sandwiches with the crusts cut off. For the first time I saw cotton growing in a field. Carl and I toasted the South with our first ever mint juleps. They slid down like lemonade, only better.

And all the while in the background, veteran contesters who had gotten into the Pillsbury made the Bake-Off sound like an audience with the Pope.

"You can't imagine what all they do for you at that one," someone said. She was right. I couldn't imagine. I thought the beef people were doing a bang-up job of keeping us all fed and entertained.

Upon registration, Carl had been given a ton of promotional material and freebies. Pot holders. Another beef apron. A ridiculously tall, Velcro-adjustable cook's hat. A dish towel printed with a cartoon Holstein howling at the moon. Recipes, recipes, recipes. The contest cookbook contained a brief rundown on each finalist along with the recipe that had won him or her a place in the contest. Those people and their methods of cooking were Carl's competition. In the privacy of our hotel room, he and I went page by page, trying to gauge his recipe's chances when weighed against such creations as Taco Ole Beef 'N' Rice, Captain's Table Rolled Roast with Blackship Glaze, Breezy Fiesta Beef Salad, and Not Your Regular Brisket. The recipes were elaborate. One man (yes, plenty of men enter these things) called for seven marrow bones cut to seven inches long and then halved lengthwise, fourteen pieces in all. These were ancillary to his five-pound chuck roast and were stacked log-cabin style in the pan under the main event and ultimately thrown away. There seemed to be no restraints on calories or fuss or cost. Twenty-two of the fifty recipes called for tenderloin or sirloin. This sort of bugged me. Well, obviously, I thought, you can make a good meal by throwing a ton of money at the ingredients. When the sky's the limit, where's the challenge?

As it turns out, I wasn't alone. Later, in the lounge downstairs, a CowBelle from Louisiana took a look at the contest booklet, snorted at the extravagance of some entries, and declared with the practicality of someone who has cooked a lot of meals for a lot of hungry ranchers, "Well, honey, in my opinion, all's you need to make a piece of tenderloin come out good is a little heat and some salt and pepper."

Lest anyone think the National Beef Cook-Off is a small-time operation, it should be known that Julia Child judged the event in 1977 and James Beard signed up for the task in 1982. Among the ten judges in Jackson were food editors from *McCall's*, *Family Circle*, the *Baltimore Sun*, and *Southern Living*. The contest began in the early sixties in Alabama and went national in 1974, although even at that only twelve states participated and it was held in a Denver high school home economics room. The next year the number of states grew to thirty-one and the next to thirty-five.

The event was structured on Pillsbury's model, which dates back to 1949. In both contests, home cooks submit recipes by mail; an independent agency sifts out the most promising submissions; and finalists win expense-paid trips to the cook-off, where as many little kitchens as there are cooks are set up with a stove and a work counter each. No sinks. Water fetching and washup occur "offstage" and are the responsibility of the assistants. Judges are food editors or cookbook authors or food experts of some sort. They are hidden away, guaranteeing fairness and anonymity; they see only the contestants' ID numbers, their printed recipes, and the finished dish. Around the edges of this are elaborate banquets and entertainment to keep everyone happily distracted.

Flipping through the booklet, I was sorry to see that rationality—or at least my idea of what's rational—was not factored into selecting finalists' recipes. Carl and I take pride in the fact that we can make a good meal without dirtying a ton of dishes, jacking up our cholesterol count, taking out a loan for ingredients, or waterlogging ourselves with salt. One woman used an entire stick of butter for her tenderloin roast. Someone else called for a full cup of sugar. The man from West Virginia marinated his sirloin steak strips in a cup of corn oil, then deep-fried them in four cups more of the stuff. This he served over mixed vegetables that had been stir-fried in still another cup. The corn oil industry must have been over the moon to see those quantities.

Not counting the man who called for canned Veg-All and mushroom soup, or the woman who squeezed liquid margarine into the bilge of her cooking pot, many of the cooks had created recipes that looked innovative and downright delicious. It was the year of the three-colored garnish. Yellow, green, and red peppers were everywhere. Cilantro, though new to many American cooks then, was well represented. Clearly, we were among people who knew what to do in the kitchen.

And there were garnishes. Ellen Burr, who ended up winning the top prize for her Beef à l'Orange, laid an onion brush along each of her four tenderloin steaks. She was not alone in specifying this greenery. Three others called for the same. (Onion brushes, for the uninitiated, are made by cutting off the root end of a scallion and discarding most of the green top. Slits are then cut into the length of the green end and the whole thing is plunged into ice water to encourage the leaves to curl and twist. Nowadays, they are beyond passé, as are radish roses. Too overwrought.)

Garnishes were no small matter in this arena, a science in themselves, since points are given for appearance. The contest people supplied neutral white plates and platters for everyone's presentation. Among other accoutrements on this plain crockery were strawberry fans, kiwi slices, an onion "chrysanthemum," an orange "chrysanthemum," apple slices dipped in cinnamon, citrus rinds in various configurations, purple edible flowers, mint sprigs, fresh oregano sprigs, lemon balm, and, of course, the ever-present classic: carrot curls. Twenty recipes called for parsley; five specified cherry tomatoes in halves or whole; five more called for full-blown tomato roses. There were fluted mushroom caps, sprinkles of grated cheese, dollops of cream, dustings of paprika, and strips of pimiento laid meticulously in little Xs.

I took all this in. As a registered guest of one of the contestants, I was authorized to wander the cooking floor during the entire frenzy of preparation among the fifty micro kitchens, as were members of the press. Aromas of every description wafted into each other. Looking around at what the more experienced cooks were turning out, I realized how incredibly naïve I was. Carl worked valiantly at his station with his CowBelle at his side. He did his best to rise to the occasion, but in truth, his pot roast looked like—well, pot roast. Humble, with steamed Brussels sprouts cut into hemispheres for his garnish. I knew how good the results probably tasted and that it was an easy, economical dish to prepare.

In the end, I began to realize that this business of cooking contests was about much more than just stirring up something good to eat. I was starting to discover how much else was involved, not the least of which were our differences about what's practical, what's wholesome, and the range of values we had all brought to the table.

CHAPTER TWO

Like me, Carl often has a hard time loosening up. For the cook-off recipe booklet, he had summed himself up conservatively by sticking to his career accomplishments in a terse bio. He said that he'd been a professor of geography at the Ohio State University and the University of Washington. He had served on an international commission for standards on digital mapping. Then he became a research manager for a company that developed software for geophysical exploration. That was all he gave them. I'm pretty much the only person who gets to see him dancing around the kitchen or bursting into a rendition of "Old Man River." Throw on a CD of the Kingsmen belting out "Louie Louie," though, and anyone around will witness Carl Youngmann in spontaneous rock 'n' roll mode. On some fronts there's no holding the man back.

He could have filled out his bio by saying he had his own KitchenAid mixer back when mixers like that were a specialty item. He cared early on about making good bread. That avocado green appliance was one of the two reasons I fell in love with him. The other was his utter lack of interest in spectator sports. No Monday Night Football at our house. He can also fix just about anything mechanical; he always knows how to pick out the best boards at the lumberyard; and he has the greatest-looking thighs in North America.

As it turned out Carl was in good company with the beef contenders. He rubbed shoulders with a hog farmer, a drill press operator, an offset printer, a home economist, and a professor of psychology who had served on two presidential commissions on mental health. There was also a psychiatrist.

Including Carl's Ph.D., at least seven of the fifty finalists held advanced degrees. Nineteen listed involvement with volunteer activities; nine mentioned gardening as a hobby; eleven put down needlework. Three said they liked to spend time shopping. Twenty finalists were contest veterans, including four who had been to the Pillsbury Bake-Off. One of these had taken the grand prize at that event.

Only one finalist listed herself as an out-and-out homemaker.

Any assumptions I might have had about who goes to these things were shattered. Clearly, the group of finalists formed a cross-section of America. They weren't a bunch of apple-cheeked ladies in gingham aprons, that's for sure. First-place winner Ellen Burr, listed foraging and mycology among her interests.

A retired librarian, she chaired her local arts council and was a member of a conservation commission. She had earned a bachelor's degree from Radcliffe and a master's from Boston University. Accepting her $15,000 award, she indicated that part of the money would be used to buy a new stove. She seemed like someone I would want to get to know—even if she *had* won by using tenderloin steaks.

In 1989, stubbornly sticking with the pot roast theme, I returned to our state competition and won with a recipe I'd titled Cumberland Beef. I learned afterward that only 150 recipes had been submitted, from which ten became state finalists. I'd started out as one in fifteen, then moved to being one in ten. Now, at the national level, I'd be one in fifty. And those cooks from other states, theoretically, would be as good as or better than I.

Cumberland Beef earned me an expense-paid ticket to Portland, Oregon. Inspired by a sauce the British sometimes eat with ham and that my mother had made on occasion to serve with the wild ducks my brother brought home from the Nisqually Delta every fall, I simmered a chuck roast in port wine with golden raisins, chopped almonds, mustard, ginger, cloves, garlic, and orange peel.

I could have flown from Seattle to Portland, but it takes nearly as long as driving by the time you consider getting to the airport, waiting to board, baggage claim, and all the rest. Choosing to make my own way, I pointed my Mazda down Interstate 5 on September 17. Driving the 180 miles didn't have the glamour of jetting off to Mississippi, but I was happy to be going even if only to the far reaches of my own backyard. Carl couldn't come along; he had things due at work. Poring over the contest book in my hotel room alone wasn't nearly as much fun as if I'd had him with me.

Finalists had graded back on butter and cream since the Mississippi cook-off, but loin cuts still ruled. No extra credit would be given to cooks who had teased a good meal out of a pound of hamburger or had coaxed tenderness out of an economical hunk of shoulder meat.

Asian flavors were a big theme. As were onion brushes. In fact, garnishes were even more elaborate than the year before. Thirty-seven of the fifty recipes specified multiple garnishes; ten people had called for three; four people called for four; and one recipe came in with a whopping five—count 'em—*five* plate-decorating components: curly endive (or kale), radish sprouts, shredded carrot, lemon rind slivers, and radish chrysanthemums, the preparation of which involves both a bowl of ice water and the risk of a few Johnson & Johnson moments with a sharp-pointed paring knife.

Bell peppers reigned supreme. More than a third of the recipes included red, yellow, and/or green slices, rings, or chunks. One called for purple. It surprised me to see recipes that had already passed through the screening process of state-level competitions that listed margarine as an ingredient. Or powdered garlic. Or canned mushrooms. Also mystifying was the pervasive use of beef-flavored granules, broth, and consommé. The Beef Commission put no restriction on how much meat we used—only that beef be the only meat in the recipes—so why not depend on the genuine article to get the flavor?

Okay. So I'm a food snob.

I'm also impatient with fussiness. One recipe called for half a teaspoon of light corn syrup. Hardly worth slobbering up a measuring spoon for, when it seemed garden-variety granulated sugar would have been a more practical way to introduce a touch of sweetness. (One recipe achieved this with strawberry jam.) The recipe that called for two tablespoons of pancake mix for dredging marinated steaks made me wonder whether plain old all-purpose flour wouldn't have gotten the job done just as well.

In the contest booklet, everyone's picture appeared above his or her bio. My smiling face lit up the left side of page 28. At the last minute, Carl had captured my image on black-and-white film on the deck of our house in the woods. In my tiny portrait I'm wearing my all-occasion uniform of a cotton turtleneck and crewneck sweater. I had removed my glasses for vanity's sake.

The bios were written in third person. Mine mentioned the geography degree I earned at the University of Washington, combined with mapping and graphic arts courses. I hadn't given the contest people much else to work with; I always get gummed up when it comes to describing myself. I suppose I like to be recognized as much as anyone, but I do not automatically step to the front. I've had a scatter of jobs ranging from underling in a brain research lab to dental assistant to graphic designer, but none of them fall into a neat pattern or career trajectory. Carl and I met in 1974 over our mutual interest in cartography. I designed maps for a while. Then we morphed our focus into graphic software development when personal computers became a reality. By the time of the Beef Cook-Off, my daughter, Karen, was twenty-four and out on her own and I was more or less retired. Not in the dot-com sense of incredible wealth, just in the lucky sense of not having to work to maintain the modest standard of living that Carl was willing to provide.

If I were to reveal the juicy bits of my history I'd have to mention the two failed marriages and maybe the long bout of depression that came close to getting me hospitalized. But that's not what the contest organizers wanted when they asked me to tell about myself in the space of six ruled lines. They wanted hobbies, fun facts, notable cooking successes. I could have said, by way of defining myself, that I don't golf or aspire to owning a yacht. I could have said my first political involvements had me doorbelling for Eugene McCarthy and crusading for the Commonwealth of Massachusetts to legalize birth control in 1969. I could have said my biologist grandfather sailed to the Antarctic on a Yankee whaling ship and became an early champion of the Marine Mammal Protection Act as a result of his voyage. He oriented me to the natural world. But when it comes down to it, I feel at a loss when distinguishing my background from other middle-aged, middle-class American women. I'm medium height, with medium coloring. My experiences overlap with a lot of other people's.

In Portland, after the cooking frenzy, after the aromas of garlic and cumin and lemon and onion and curry had dissipated into the HVAC system of the Red Lion Inn's grand ballroom, after my efforts at Cumberland Beef were a done deal and the judges' decisions would be final, our entertainment splash was a bus trip to a nearby cattle ranch for an evening rodeo, my first time seeing bucking broncos, calf roping, and bull riding in the flesh. It was a four-star event. As temporary VIPs we all seemed to have front-row seats.

Some people don't approve of rodeos, claiming cruelty to animals. I can see their point. On the other hand, we weren't exactly a crowd of vegetarians or PETA activists. This event was brought to us by the people who raise, slaughter, butcher, and sell meat, after all. And we, as cooks, were there as supposed experts at putting it on the plate.

I should say that Carl and I are not very dedicated carnivores. I'm one of those people who actually *likes* to tuck into a jiggling mass of tofu on occasion. Maybe three nights a week we go meatless at our house, although I didn't volunteer this detail to the ranchers who were wining and dining me. When I see someone drape a steak the size of Montana across a platter, I sometimes pull back and reconsider the possibility of going vegetarian.

The key is not focusing on what meat really is. Some years ago I shopped in a swanky California market. The butcher had his own names for his cuts of meat. Envisioning one of those dashed-line charts of a steer in profile to identify the round, the chuck, the shank, and the fore shank, I pointed through the glass case and asked which muscle mass one of the roasts had been taken from.

"Oh, that was never any muscle," the butcher said. "Or if it was, it was one the animal never used."

I suppose he was trying to make the roast sound more tender and appealing. But what did he think meat was if not muscle? I pictured a bunch of cows flopping around in sunglasses on chaise longues and with pink straws in polka-dot lemonade glasses in a daisy field, graciously waiting their turn at the abattoir.

Baxter Black, the cowboy poet and former large animal veterinarian of National Public Radio fame, had been hired as host and emcee for the awards ceremony our second night in Portland. As an entertainer, he fit right in with the ranchers, and he knew just how to tease a smile out of most of the cooks. I confess I had never heard of the guy until that weekend. But suddenly, right there in the lobby of that convention center hotel, a Cow Belle I knew from Washington, who apparently was acquainted with this feisty little poet and his enormous mustache, caught the two of us in close proximity. She wanted a picture of him giving me a squeeze. We obliged. The flashbulb went off. And in the heat of the moment he planted a kiss on my cheek. Funny when strangers feign intimacy for the sake of the Kodak moment. I'm not usually that spontaneous, but there you go. I kept my copy of the photo, too.

Baxter mellowed up the crowd, and then it was time for the contestants to parade across the stage as the next act. The idea was for us to line up from Alabama to Wyoming, step forward to face the audience one by one, and say something clever about our home states. I couldn't think of a single amusing thing to say about Washington that hadn't been said a million times before. Rain? Slugs? D. B. Cooper, the world's first in-flight hijacker?

Whatever I did stumble out I've blocked from my memory. I'm just such a dud when it comes to being fun on demand.

And I was also a dud at capturing any of the prizes. I didn't especially have my heart set on winning but I guess I'd have to admit to disappointment when Baxter Black failed to call me forward on the stage. I thought my Cumberland Beef was pretty good. It's so ingrained in me, however, to put on the face of a good loser that I can usually make myself believe I didn't care. The experience alone was worth plenty, and I concentrated on that. There's an art to being left in the dust while still smiling. Someday I hope to perfect that.

The Beef Commission was hosting three competitions that weekend in Portland. In addition to my Indoor Cooking division, with fifty cooks from fifty states, there was also an Outdoor Barbecue division and a Microwave division, with seven regional finalists each. Top prize in each division was $5,000. From the three first-place winners, one would be awarded a bonus of $10,000 for best overall.

Best of Beef—the grand prize—went to Linda Wright from Medford Lakes, New Jersey, for her Mexican Flank Steak with Mock Tamales. It looked hugely complicated with marinating and barbecuing and two subrecipes, one for Linda's Sassy Salsa and the other for the Mock Tamales, which consisted of two kinds of grated cheese rolled up in flour tortillas with some minced green onion that were then wrapped individually in foil and tucked into the edge of a charcoal fire. They seemed more like quesadillas than tamales to me. The salsa called for two plum tomatoes to be finely chopped and three plum tomatoes to be coarsely chopped. I probably would have given all five a medium cut, but who knows? Linda Wright might have been on to something.

The head judge was Dotty Griffith, food editor of the *Dallas Morning News*. She said of Ms. Wright's creation, "From the moment it hit the judges' table, we knew this was something that had tremendous consumer appeal.... the great taste outweighed any of the inconvenience."

Mary Lou Newhouse from Vermont won $5,000 in the Indoor category for her Harvest Thyme Beef Sandwiches. The possibility of a sandwich taking first place had not occurred to me, probably because I'm not much of a bread/meat/bread enthusiast myself. I took another look at her recipe and had to admit that it did seem refreshing—something of a standout from all the heavy stuff the rest of us had made. I bet the judges liked the crunch of her shredded raw turnip and carrot. I bet they appreciated the conviction of her horseradish. Those are things I like myself but hadn't thought of.

Media people had been swarming the place. Since the main thrust of this three-day jamboree was promotion of an industry, members of the press were welcomed into the party.

Erik Lacitis from the *Seattle Times* began a conversation with me by asking what my favorite seasoning was. Oregano, I said. Then we talked about *epazote*, a Mexican herb he was unfamiliar with. I told him where to find it in Seattle, and that completed our interview.

Jonathan Susskind, who had recently been hired as the food

editor at the *Seattle Post-Intelligencer*, went a little deeper. I sat with him in the hotel lobby. He was new to Washington so we chatted a bit about relocation and the Northwest. He said he hadn't found a good cup of coffee in all of Portland. I liked his fuchsia sweater.

His article the following Wednesday said, "One could meet folks among the 1,000 industry promoters, contestants, media and ranchers who claimed they could eat beef every day and never tire of it. But in the majority were those who admitted that after four days of beefy lunches and dinners, a poached chicken breast sounded tasty....Mathews confessed that after only a couple of days, she snuck out for lunch to a nearby Vietnamese restaurant....Mathews' Cumberland Beef was a comfort-food dish...I thought it was pretty tasty and really simple, but one judge later said the platter looked drab and the taste was ordinary."

I drove back to Seattle as I'd driven down, no richer, no poorer. A tiny bit smarter, though. A carton of clean cooking utensils rattled in the trunk of my car. Passing I-5 exits to Kalama, Cathlamet, Kelso, Castle Rock, I let my mind wander in the direction of what could be done with a piece of beef that hadn't been done before. Maybe tenderloin after all. Or a new kind of stir-fry for next year's contest. Or something Middle Eastern. Eggplant? Something less drab. Less ordinary.

CHAPTER THREE

With a few of my contest successes featured in the local papers and a couple of small prizes under my belt, word had gotten out. Acquaintances began to assume I was some kind of fabulous cook, which I am not. I'm an adequate cook. I don't fuss; I refuse to buy extravagant ingredients. I'm a get-dinner-on-the-table cook. There's not much I know to do in the kitchen that you couldn't look up in the second edition of the *Joy of Cooking*.

My mother relied on Irma Rombauer's first edition. I remember the kitchen where I grew up and that the shelf to the right of the stove had been designed by my parents' architect to accommodate my mother's store of seasonings, nearly every product put out by the Spice Islands company in the fifties. Like little glass soldiers, those straight-sided jars of anise and coriander and summer savory, tarragon, chervil, marjoram, caraway, and all the rest, with their distinctive brown caps and red-printed labels, seemed somehow like keys on a flavor piano, each combination resulting in a unique chord that only my mother knew how to play. She did not teach me to cook.

As an adolescent I was allowed to explore the inner workings of the fridge, the pantry, and the Mixmaster if I felt inspired to try my hand at occasional cakes and cookies, as long as I cleaned up after myself, didn't ask for help, and accepted the household standard of substituting whole wheat flour for white and raw sugar or molasses for what my mother called "white death," the granulated stuff. My mother also had myriad, not-so-subtle ways to remind me to go light on the butter. Walnuts, too, were closely monitored. Maybe this stinginess was a leftover from her having lived through the Depression. Ours was a family of seven, and although my father was a physician, money always seemed tight. Maybe the butter obsession was the residual effect of World War II rationing. I remember going with my mother in the early fifties to the far side of town where a special butcher would sell her horse meat. Those purchases may have been related to scarcity of other meats. Or economizing. Or both. Or maybe my mother and father simply liked the purple flesh. As for eschewing refined foods, my parents had gone whole-hog into the back-to-the-land craze of the forties. Before moving our family to Olympia, Washington, they had kept a small farm in Connecticut with goats, sheep, a one-eyed horse named Judy, a giant garden, and chickens in the yard. My mother, who held an English degree from Vassar, slaughtered, rendered, and butchered; she put up quarts of beans and tomatoes. My father had graduated from Phillips Exeter Academy, Princeton College, Harvard Medical School and had taught at Yale. In spite of all that ivy, he liked nothing better than the simplicity of driving his Army-surplus jeep as a tractor, cutting hay or tilling the soil.

A generation later, I would have my own turn at going back to the land, when I, too, would milk goats as my mother had. Adelle Davis would become my idol and, like my mother, I would sprinkle brewer's yeast in nearly everything except my tea. I, too, would come to believe in the benefits of whole grains.

As a new bride at age eighteen I had two concerns when it came to running my own kitchen. First, I was mystified about how to get the pork chops, the boiled potatoes, and the green beans all to come out ready at the same time. And second, I didn't know how to flavor anything except cinnamon toast.

While my mother may have failed to teach me anything explicit in the nature of meal preparation, she did me a great service. With the unearned confidence of youth, I bought every herb and spice whose names were familiar to me, words I'd grown up hearing all my life. Cardamom, sage, oregano, thyme, turmeric, basil, rosemary, and of course cinnamon. I lined up their unmatched boxes and jars to the side of my stove and began to cook by smell. Depending on what I'd be preparing that night, I'd open my seasonings one by one, sniffing each intently until arriving at the one that smelled right for what I was making. Eventually I learned that thyme goes with chicken, sage with pork, and so on, all modeled on my mother's own kitchen practices and the meals I'd grown up tasting. In the end, she had taught by example, which was not that bad a way to learn, a sort of olfactory Braille. As a result I am gutsy and experimental at the stove. While I take almost no physical risks and am profoundly timid in other facets of daily life, I lack the normal fear of working without a net when it comes to playing with my food.

IN 1992, while shopping at Safeway, I noticed ten-pound bags of Pillsbury Best flour with promotions for the thirty-fifth Bake-Off printed on the front. I grabbed a bag and plopped it into my cart. At home, I rushed the ice cream into the freezer but did not settle the milk into the fridge or the potatoes and onions into their bins before reading every single word of the contest's fine print.

I'd heard of the Bake-Off all my life but knew nothing of the particulars until that day. I remembered those women in Kenne-wick who had said, "At the Pillsbury they treat you like a queen, a real queen."

I was three years old in 1949 when Pillsbury first staged its Grand National Recipe and Baking Contest, as they called it in the beginning. The media shortened the name right away to Bake-Off for practical purposes. The name stuck and is now a registered trademark of the company. The contest was held at the Waldorf-Astoria Hotel in New York City. The idea was to pamper one hundred of America's best home cooks with breakfast in bed, pheasant under glass, and big-money prizes. The award checks didn't have as many zeros as they do now, but then bread cost only 14¢ a loaf; the average house could be bought for $14,500; and the minimum wage was 40¢ an hour.

Until I saw those specially printed bags of flour on the grocery shelf, I'd had no idea of how or when one might try to become part of this wonderful, silly, wholesome morsel of Americana. It's the Olympic Games of cooking contests. I had a vague image in my head of Art Linkletter in black and white, ogling a heap of gooey cinnamon rolls and a mile-high pie. He was handing over one of those oversized cardboard checks to some lucky woman in a cap-sleeved apron, a pageboy haircut, and cat-eye glasses. My parents refused to own a television while I was growing up, so I can't say where that image came from. I simply assumed that—along with Burma Shave jingles, hula hoops, and Silly Putty—everyone was familiar with the Bake-Off as part of the quirky weave of this country's fabric. The mystery lay in how one might become selected to participate.

The rules on the bag said any resident of the United States who was age twelve or older and not engaged in the food business at a professional level could enter. No proof of purchase was required and we could enter as many times as we liked. Each recipe had to be original to its sender, had to be mailed separately in its own envelope, and had to include at least one of the qualifying ingredients; these were listed, with specific minimum amounts. The company began milling wheat in 1869. Since then, however, it had expanded to produce other edibles such as cake and brownie mixes and the refrigerated doughs that come in paper tubes to make automatic biscuits, cinnamon rolls, and pizza crusts. Pillsbury was also in charge of the Green Giant and his line of vegetables, both frozen and canned.

The ingredients list and their amounts sounded eminently workable for the most part. I couldn't wait to stage my attack on the bag of flour I'd bought. Carl and I were living then in the country on the outskirts of Seattle. We had a big airy house with a big bright kitchen. That expanse of counter space cried out for me to start experimenting.

Since all-purpose flour was what got the whole thing started at the Waldorf-Astoria, and since I'm generally what you'd call a from-scratch cook, I shied away from the convenience foods on the list.

I went at the problem much as I would have approached a design project: What are we trying to accomplish? What do we have to work with? What are the constraints? I say *we* because I always have the feeling Carl is backing me. He's a great sounding board when I'm ready to talk through my ideas.

In retrospect, I don't think I was approaching the recipe invention process in quite the right spirit. I might have been overly rigid. Too analytical. No passion. Or I might have been trying too hard. I reviewed the list of ingredients. I didn't for a minute consider fooling around with boil-in-the-bag frozen rice with peas and mushrooms; frozen pasta with broccoli, corn, and carrots in garlic-seasoned sauce; or broccoli in cheese-flavored sauce. They seemed more foreign to me than the Vietnamese *nuoc mam* and mung bean noodles I keep on the shelf. Besides, the idea of packaging and shipping cooked rice and pasta around the country goes against my nature. Rice and noodles keep indefinitely on the pantry shelf and require nothing more than boiling when the time comes.

I considered the difference between making something with the goal of winning or making something with the goal of having something to eat. After all, some of the recipes that had made it to the top in previous Bake-Offs either used a bunch of ridiculous ingredients or they were jam-packed with salt or fat. When my daughter was little I overheard her tell a playmate one day, "Grease scares my mother." And she was right.

I decided to cook the way I would ordinarily cook, with ingredients I understood. A frozen pea, for example, is something I relate to. So I laid in a supply just in case innovation struck. Then I relented and bought my first ever box of Pillsbury's prefab pie crusts and tucked them into the door of my fridge, just in case.

Since we're a nation of bread eaters, I started out in search of a new and different loaf. That's when I realized how hard it is to think of anything that hasn't already been done by someone somewhere who has more imagination than I do.

In the end I generated a baker's dozen recipes to submit, beginning with banana muffins. They were an adaptation of some I'd been making for years; I added miller's bran and orange marmalade. Right off the bat, I choked up when it came to naming things. I don't know how much difference it makes in the judging to have a clever name, but it felt almost like a matter of self-respect to send in something with a name that was both descriptive and creative. I admire people who can come up with great names, as Karin Fellows did for her Split Seconds cookies, and Karen Durrett for naming her Mexican/Italian pizzas Chicken and Black Bean Tostizzas. Ellen Burr, of the Beef Cook-Off fame, named her 1990 entry Dotted Swiss and Spinach Quiche. The brilliance of that name is that she topped her quiche with a generous sprinkle of sesame seeds, which were, in fact, suggestive of the dots on dotted Swiss fabric, while the name also referenced the Swiss cheese in the recipe.

Peanut Blossoms, Tunnel of Fudge, Ring-a-Lings. Crisps, twists, winks, snaps. I looked my muffins in the eye. They were brown. They were functional. So I typed the utilitarian name Banana Nut Muffins at the top of the page and moved on.

WOULD a plain name hurt my chances at success? I hoped not. I wanted to believe the recipes themselves were what counted most. Rather than agonize over titles, I kept going in the kitchen, knowing for certain that none of my names would incorporate the words *Fiesta* or *Zesty* or *Easy* or *Choco* or *'N'* as in something *'n'* something.

It turned out that Ellen Anders would win a prize with her Great Northern Bean Stew. Can you get more magnificently matter-of-fact than that? It's both descriptive and straightforward. Like her, I decided to stick with the safe and easy approach.

I submitted Curry Dinner Rolls, spiced dough rolled around plain yogurt, chopped peanuts, and green onions. Next came Gingerbread Dumplings with Lemon Sauce, Chocolate Almond Coffee Ring, Herbed Baguettes, Corsican Flatbread, and Orange Walnut Bread.

By then I was ready to tackle the frozen peas, from which I concocted Garden Green Fresh Pea Soup, an eye-popping chartreuse puree seasoned with mint, cumin, turmeric, garlic, ginger and fleshed out with carrot and potato. Going back to the bag of flour, I came up with Nutmeg Pancakes with Apple Pie Syrup, which I can still heartily recommend.

Then I dug deeper and splurged on a Pillsbury hot roll mix. I added three eggs to the dough for a brioche-like texture, broke off walnut-sized globs and rolled them in a blend of instant coffee, cocoa, sugar, and chopped almonds. These I heaped in a loaf pan to bake. I called them Mocha Almond Pull-Aparts.

Then I dug deeper still. And I suppose this is where Pillsbury wanted me to go in the first place when they'd created their list of qualifying ingredients. I bought a tube of refrigerated biscuits, whacked the paper can against the edge of my kitchen counter, flattened the circles of dough to within an inch of their lives, and slathered them with olive oil, fresh garlic, poppy seeds, rosemary, oregano, and fresh-ground black pepper, then baked them to a crisp. Those I called Italian Cracker Bread and entered them in the Quick Ideas category.

The rules outlined four cooking categories with no limit on number of entries: Quick Ideas, Special Treats, Light and

Healthy Creations, and Ethnic Specialties. It was up to me to slot my entries accordingly. Did I mention the Hazelnut Sesame Bread? That went into Light and Healthy.

All the while there were those two prefab pie crusts lurking in my fridge and reminding me of their red-box presence every time I opened the door. A dessert pie seemed too obvious to try for and not part of my usual repertoire anyway. So I went for something savory and came up with the recipe to end all recipes. Or so I thought. Mashed potato pie. That's not what I called it, but that was the concept. And I'll willingly admit it makes for something of a marketing challenge, because the thought of potatoes in pie crust doesn't have instant appeal. The concept made me laugh at myself. In the old comic strip, Dagwood Bumstead would open his lunchbox to find that his wife, Blondie, had made him yet another mashed potato sandwich, a joke about the lowest of low cuisine. But consider that my creation had sautéed leeks and crumbled Roquefort and plenty of eggs to enrich it, and lots of chopped fresh chives and parsley and a generous sprinkling of grated nutmeg—really, I didn't see how anyone could resist—especially after I titled it Vichyssoise Roquefort Supper Pie. Okay, that's a bit of a mouthful. But it's descriptive.

In my defense I'd like to point out that later, in 1996, Christina Hurst would enter and win cash money with something she would boldly and baldly call Savory Mashed Potato Pie. So you see? I wasn't that far off the mark. Maybe just ahead of my time.

CHAPTER FOUR

All that cooking and I didn't hear a thing from Pillsbury. Meanwhile, Carl and I woke up to the realization that the suburbs were expanding toward our front door and that we no longer lived in the country. Since most of our friends and activities were in town, we found new homes for our sheep, ducks, and geese. We sold the house with the big bright kitchen and moved into a huge fixer-upper on Seattle's Capitol Hill, not too far from where we had started our married life.

It was September 1992, and we were beginning a new chapter. Our house needed everything. The furnace didn't work. The water heater gave up. Paint was actively peeling, inside and out. The stove had a short circuit that I learned of with a terrifying shock. Bathtubs weren't in the right places. Plumbing. Wiring.

Squirrels in the attic. I woke to the sound of water pouring down our bedroom wall one stormy November night. Time to tear off the old roof, buy a load of shingles, and find someone to tack them on. I wrote some gigantic checks.

Then I took a detour into the medical world. My health concerns turned out to be something of a false alarm; by the time I had recovered from my surgery, I was as good as new. But the impact of that experience paled in comparison to the blow that followed. On a rainy day tucked beneath the usual dazzle of August's stunning brightness, and with our kitchen temporarily taken down to the studs, we learned that my wonderful, funny, pretty sister had elected to end her life. There had been earlier attempts. Psychiatrists. Mood-elevating drugs, none of them successful. All the while my family and I had held her in the gentle basket of our arms. Now empty. A year apart in age, she and I had spent nearly half a century thinking of ourselves as twins. Now she had set me adrift.

In the immediate aftermath seven relatives came to stay with Carl and me. Others who lived locally drifted in and out during the day. Even our big house felt full to overflowing with a dozen or more people stirring around, a blessing really. We all wanted to be together, holding each other up. None of it felt like a burden, more like an honor that I—the youngest sibling—was trusted to provide the temporary locus for our grief. Still, with nine full-grown adults sleeping in our house, where it was usually only the two of us, it seemed I had to invent sheets and towels out of thin air, and we all had to cooperate on hot water for showers.

What I especially remember of those days was cooking and

serving. Any of us would have denied having much appetite to speak of. Nevertheless, we went though the motions of breakfast, lunch, and dinner.

I feel absolutely clear on why I found meal preparation to be a comfort in those hard days: It was a process I could count on. In every other respect I seemed to have lost control of my world. But in my kitchen an egg was still an egg and a loaf of bread would still cut into approximately sixteen slices, even with my sister Emeline gone. Potatoes, if put in a 350-degree oven, would be steamy and ready for butter in an hour's time. I was sure of that, and I'd rather have been baking banana muffins first thing in the morning than staring out the window and weeping. Standing at my stove—even while operating at half speed—was the one place where I had confidence in the results of my actions. I knew how to put the most basic scoop of rice, piece of fish, and green something-or-other on a dinner plate, whereas I did not know how to lose a sister.

My world had spun out of control everywhere but in my kitchen.

After the service, after everyone had returned to their own homes, after the dahlias had faded, I stumbled through days and then weeks with no clear focus. For a long while nothing seemed to matter. A friend took me to Florida to perk me up, but I couldn't tell you what we saw or where we went. Beaches, I suppose. And along the way, wherever possible—because I don't much like eating in restaurants—I cooked in city parks over the backpacking stove I'd taken with me in my duffel bag on the plane. Dicing carrots, tomatoes, parsnips, garlic, and onions for soup was a routine that felt remarkably grounding. I stirred and stirred while trying to find my place in the world again.

The following spring Carl's mother died. The morning after her church service, I made buttermilk pancakes for Carl's entire family. I didn't know of anything else I could do for them.

No sooner had we begun to deal with that loss than my mother was diagnosed with cancer. As the disease overtook her, she needed help with personal and household chores. She and I were not as close as some mothers and daughters. Nevertheless, I rubbed her feet; I tracked and dispensed her medications; I did her laundry. I put lotion on her arms.

Toward the end of her illness she became helpless. On her last morning I fixed her the world's tiniest amount of steel-cut oatmeal and put it in a blue and white bowl with brown sugar and half-and-half. I chose the shiniest silver teaspoon in the drawer. I poured two ounces of orange juice into cut crystal and placed everything on a tray lined with Irish linen along with a pewter vase that held three Shasta daisies from her garden. It turned out she was too weak to eat any of it, but I believe she appreciated the details. My mother and I had never found a comfortable level of conversational intimacy, but we shared the language of food.

Carl and I are Quakers, members of the Religious Society of Friends. In the absence of other family members having religious affiliations, planning my sister's memorial service had fallen to us. The afternoon of my mother's last day, she finally acknowledged that her condition was terminal by asking for her own service to be held in the manner of Friends. "Please do for me what you did for Emeline," she said. Then she thanked me and told me where to find her will.

With three deaths in the space of fifty-six weeks, I felt downright dazed and rubbery. It took a long while to begin to come back into daylight.

In late February 1996, I remember the distinct moment of being on my hands and knees, grouting ceramic tiles on our kitchen floor, when the radio announced the outcome of the thirty-seventh Pillsbury Bake-Off. Kurt Wait of Redwood City, California, had flavored a chocolate cake mix with cinnamon and combined the batter with a can of sliced pears, then slathered the results with a jar of butterscotch caramel ice-cream topping. Nice move, I thought (except perhaps for the caramel). Clever to use pears and not the more expected apples. His inclusion of macadamia nuts seemed a good touch as well. Who needs walnuts anymore? So passé.

I wanted to do something clever myself. I determined not to miss out the next time the contest rolled around. Carl, my biggest supporter in all things creative, teased me about opening the test kitchens.

FOR its first twenty-seven years the Bake-Off was held annually, but the mega-huge scale of staging the event grew to seam-splitting proportions. In 1976 Pillsbury had gone to a two-year cycle. In 1996 when Kurt Wait showed up to bake his Macadamia Fudge Torte in Dallas and slice off a few gooey slabs for the judges to wolf down, the grand prize had grown, too. He was the first man to take highest honors and the first ever to win a million dollars for home cooking.

The summer of 1997 Carl agreed to a five-week consulting contract in Brisbane, Australia, and I was going along. Our daughter, Karen, was pregnant, but it was early enough in the pregnancy that she would be able to join us for two of those weeks.

In the twenty-five years that I'd known him, Carl had migrated from being a university professor to a graphic software developer to managing the mapping unit for a geophysical company to managing the software development for an automated Pap smear analysis system. The common thread in his work was image processing. Whether from a satellite or a digital microscope, all pictures can be reduced to measures of tone, texture, shape, pattern, and edges. With my own—but more limited—experience in mapping and remote sensing, I liked having a basic understanding of Carl's work. While employed by the Pap smear company, however, he shifted away from engineering and into the deep, dark world of government regulation. He became a specialist in applying for FDA approval and putting medical devices on the market. I didn't know the first thing about that. The gig in Brisbane was a clinical trial. I was going along not as a work partner but as a wife, pure and simple. He'd have two weeks to kill between setting up the trial and verifying the resulting data.

The only problem in preparing for the trip was that the Bake-Off submission deadline would occur a few days after our return. With the hefty time difference and the twenty-seven hours of air travel, I couldn't begin to predict what condition I'd be in after arriving home. Before packing my snorkel for the Great Barrier Reef, I went into high gear in the kitchen and started writing recipes.

The list of qualifying ingredients for the 1998 contest included a couple of real doozies. Underwood deviled ham and B&M baked beans stood out as challenges. The ham spread was beyond anything I felt ready to approach, given that it's almost three-quarters fat. On the belief, however, that extra credit might be granted for rising to the test, I bought a can of beans, opened it, gave it a sniff, and waited for inspiration to strike. It was my first voluntary contact with a baked bean in approximately half a lifetime. I can't say why I started there. Any of the other ingredients would have made more sense.

But, hey, anything's possible. Just as Carl and I had learned about the Beef Cook-Off when we attended the Western Washington State Fair in Puyallup, while there we had also stopped at the Northwest Dry Pea & Bean Commission display. It so happens that farmers around the Palouse Hills near the Idaho border have such success raising brown lentils that they not only sell them all over the United States, but they export them to India. At the booth Carl and I had taste-tested all kinds of things made with the lens-shaped legumes. Chili, soup, salsa, and...lentil brownies, which were, amazingly, not half bad. I took a copy of the recipe and made them at home. They were a pain to put together, however. The lentils had to be cooked first, then mashed before incorporating them into the batter.

With the open can of beans staring me in the face, I thought, why not try a riff on the same general idea? The beans were already cooked; that would save a step. The Japanese put all kinds of legumes into their sweets. Adzuki beans, red bean paste. And these brownies were going to be terrifically nutritious.... Besides, what I don't like about canned baked beans is how sweet they are. In a dessert bar, that would be an asset. I mashed beans and made some batter. But not too much.

Much as an artist will work in thumbnail sketches when trying out an idea, I do the same when developing a recipe. I work in the smallest possible proportions. I think of it as sketching, not committing myself until I have a rough sense of whether the idea has merit. But even at a quarter recipe those brownies—more like blondies, since they incorporated no chocolate—sat on the counter for days. Scott Hacker, an orthopedic surgeon who was renting a room from us for the first year of his residency and who sucked up food like a vacuum cleaner each time he passed through the kitchen, didn't touch them. I took this as a sign. And, surely, even if they had been good, this wasn't the sort of thing Pillsbury would be awarding prizes for. No sex appeal.

With my thumbnail approach, I had failed to empty the can of beans, however. My New England grandmother, bless her, instilled in me that one simply does not throw out food in good conscience. She was known to thicken soup with leftover oatmeal.

In the interests of full disclosure, I'll confess to my next move and get it over with, although I'll probably live to regret making this public: I made cole slaw with baked beans and chopped peanuts mixed in.

I forget which part of this sounded as if it would be good, although I make no apology for having experimented. As I learned in the software business, a test is not a test until you break what's being tested. You can't find the limit without exceeding it. I didn't try this stuff out on Carl, my A-1 taste tester. The man is almost too easygoing for his own good, and he's willing to eat just about anything. But.

The trick with inspiration is to get to the edge of what works and not a millimeter beyond. As I found in graphic design, there are a thousand "right" answers to most creative problems. What you want is that perfect balance: something completely familiar combined with elements never before imagined. The results should appear effortless, recognizable while still seeming new.

The only way I know of finding that creative edge is to straddle it, suffer failure, and cross my fingers for the occasional success. And who's ever going to know about whatever I bungle along the way anyway? My kitchen is private territory and the risks are pretty small. It's not as if we're talking about anyone being poisoned, and my disposal was in good working order, ready to receive the cole slaw. It was that bad.

The big challenge for me when trying to generate ideas is to grab the first impulse of inspiration before the potential of an *aha* moment evaporates. Those moments are the raw material of creativity. Of course, those inspirations don't always pan out. My next act was to boil a couple of canned biscuits to see what would happen. After all, bagels and pretzels are boiled before baking. But the results were embarrassingly white, soggy, and tasteless.

Not ready to give up entirely, I stirred up a sauce of butter, sugar, cinnamon, and flour with a cup or so of apple juice, brought it to a simmer, floated the remainder of the biscuits in it, covered, and steamed them over a low flame. The results were vaguely reminiscent of apple dumplings. But something was decidedly missing. Apples maybe.

The 1998 Bake-Off was the first year in its history in which Pillsbury Best flour was not a qualifying ingredient. Too bad. I feel very much at ease with—even inspired by—such a wonderfully simple start as a bag of flour. But I had twenty-seven other food products to choose from. More, if you count all the possible flavors and varieties of the frozen vegetables, canned frosting, and cake mixes that were on the list of eligible products.

Clearly, with my baked bean flops and the biscuit experiments, I had been going at this thing all wrong, trying to force an idea with too much intellectualizing and not enough intuition. I studied the list of qualifying ingredients again. I wish I could say something smart about how I came up with the ideas that eventually made it onto paper and into the mail, but it was essentially seat-of-my-pants, skin-of-my-teeth desperation. I had no idea what the judges would be looking for. Nevertheless, I kept at it, going on the belief that if you give enough monkeys enough typewriters and enough time, one of them will tap out either the complete works of Shakespeare or a recipe that every cook across America will want to adopt.

CHAPTER FIVE

Eventually I hit on the idea of deconstructing the qualifying ingredients.

I remember standing in the ethnic foods aisle of my neighborhood Safeway, studying the label on a jar of Old El Paso Thick 'n Chunky Salsa (Pillsbury owned that brand), when I realized all I had to do was start with an existing recipe that called for the same ingredients that were in that jar. Substitute the salsa for the recipe's tomatoes, onions, and jalapeños and, voilà! Reverse engineering. Quick and Easy was the theme of the contest.

I'd never cooked with bottled salsa, but the product seemed benign enough. At home I rifled through my accordion file of recipes, where I cram pages I've torn out of the newspaper or dashed off onto the backs of envelopes. Theoretically, the recipes are alphabetized, but in reality most of them are stuffed in the back. I dug around and came up with one that had parity with the salsa ingredients.

A few years before, a friend had given me his variation on Paul Prudhomme's Seafood Creole, which I had then adapted pretty strenuously myself. For example, I don't like scallops, so I left them out and increased the amounts of shrimp and halibut. I used Prudhomme's olive oil but not his butter. I never use bay leaves; they taste bitter to me. I increased the black pepper and omitted the white. After all, they both come from the same plant. I simplified Prudhomme's canned whole tomatoes, chopped fresh tomatoes, and can of tomato sauce to one can of crushed. I added okra and increased the number of shiitake mushrooms. By the time this gumbo reached my stove, it felt like my own creation.

I called the results Salsa Seafood Creole and printed two copies. One I mailed to Pillsbury and the other I tucked into the accordion file in my pantry.

By now our kitchen remodel had been completed. The butler's pantry—almost a second kitchen itself leading into our big dining room—was my favorite place in the house, with its north light and tiled green marble countertops. That room felt safe and private and solid. The window looked onto the quiet of our side garden. Carl had cleverly hung the top of an antique hutch on one wall, a piece I'd bought at an auction. For the missing glass on the doors, he used brass mesh. Then he made shelves from antique pine foundry patterns I'd bought at another auction. All that storage space put everything within reach: seasonings, baking supplies, serving dishes. Carl's old avocado green KitchenAid mixer stood on the counter, the only small appliance I leave set up. I don't like a clutter of toasters and blenders and their associated cords; those I keep in the cabinet when not in use.

That Seattle kitchen wasn't my only remodel. My first was in California in 1969. Then I returned to the Northwest to settle on ten acres, where I set about realizing my fantasy of Earth-mother organic self-sufficiency with chickens, goats, pigs, sheep, and an old apple orchard. The kitchen there wasn't fancy, but it was big enough for me to process what I'd raised. I even had room to experiment with making my own cheese.

In our thirty-two years together Carl and I have owned and occupied five houses. We've remodeled four of those kitchens. When I cook I generally spread out, so I always go for installing base cabinets a few inches out from the wall to allow for extra-deep counters. This precludes buying ready-made countertops, but that's okay; I like to set tile. I also like quick access to bowls and pans and plates, so I prefer a kitchen with open shelves rather than upper cabinets. As for color trends, I've never bought an appliance or plumbing fixture that wasn't white. (Years ago a designer friend made the point that white is always in style and her point stuck.) In terms of luxury, I've never felt the need for more than one oven and four gas burners. Anything beyond that would confuse me. Those faux restaurant stoves strike me as just a wee bit scary. Blowtorch cooking isn't my thing.

In addition to the kitchens we've remodeled, we built one

from the ground up, as part of a remote cabin on the east slope of the Cascade Mountains. We made the place with our own four hands beginning with a laid-up stone foundation. Carl chainsawed the structural members from trees that had been growing on the property. There I cooked on a woodstove, pioneer style, learning to regulate the heat of the fire, the dampers, and the drafts. I roasted more than one turkey in that cast-iron oven, made bread, baked cookies. During the summer, however, in an effort not to overheat the cabin's interior, I kindled a small fire and quick-cooked whatever I could on the stovetop. This led to a variety of desserts that are inelegantly called *slumps* and *grunts*, cake batter cooked over some sort of stewed fruit or sweet sauce in a covered pan.

Whether from laziness or practicality, I've always been somewhat intrigued by the idea of cakes that don't need frosting and pies that don't need crusts. In other words, I want a gooey dessert without the fuss or calories. So with the woodstove experiences in mind, I tried a stovetop cake with a Pillsbury mix. Chocolate batter steamed on chocolate sauce. Assuming other cooks would appreciate a self-frosting cake, I submitted the recipe, something of an upside-down arrangement by the time I tilted it out of the pan and onto a plate. It didn't have eye appeal in the least, a brown-on-brown heap impossible to dress up or garnish. But it ate well. It was easy to assemble, and the cleanup was a snap.

The problem I have with cake mixes, however, is that the results are often too sweet and too soft for my taste; they're overleavened, not dense enough. So I tried toning down a plain yellow cake mix with added flour, rolled oats, dried fruit, and nuts; I scented the batter with cardamom. From this I made free-form drop muffins. They were good enough to eat. I submitted them under the name of Sunday Tea Cakes.

Then I reworked my frozen pea soup from the last time I'd entered the contest and submitted that one also.

A few days before we left for Australia, I cleared out the freezer. In the back a near-empty bag of skinless, boneless chicken thighs rattled around. In the fridge was the half-empty bottle of salsa, left over from the Seafood Creole. Again I let my mind wander.

CHAPTER SIX

Once I sink my teeth into a puzzle I'm hooked. You might say I was obsessed with recipe daydreaming. I couldn't let go of the notion of reverse engineering—deconstructing that bottle of salsa, in other words—as a way of getting myself into this contest.

One more time, I rifled through my accordion file of recipes looking for a takeoff point. That's when I came across a clipping from the *Seattle Times*: Braised Halibut with Middle Eastern Spices. Perfect. It called for tomatoes, onions, and garlic. Why not substitute chicken for fish, I thought, and substitute olive oil for vegetable oil? That would lend the recipe an air of authenticity. I left out the cayenne because the salsa was already piquant. To underscore the ethnic theme, I added chopped almonds and dried currants. Cinnamon and cumin eased the salsa's flavor gracefully but firmly away from its Mexican origins and into the Moroccan realm.

All of this I made in half quantity. That's how much chicken I had to use up. I didn't have couscous, the logical complement, so I steamed some white rice. Carl and I both thought the results were pretty good. So two days before leaving on a five-week adventure, I uncharacteristically made a special trip to Safeway for the express purpose of buying more chicken thighs. I wavered over whether a serving should be one thigh or two. Giving in to big American appetites, I went with two, and bought eight to make four servings. I also bought couscous.

At home I scaled the recipe up to full size. Scott Hacker, our renter, and by now our friend, cruised through at just the right moment to prevent me from worrying about leftovers. He was an enthusiastic eater.

Sometimes, inexplicably, the seasonings need adjusting when you double or halve a recipe. Not in this case. I wrote it up as I'd made it, with no alteration from the first round save for the doubling of everything. I typed up the recipe and gave it the unimaginative name of Salsa Couscous Chicken. Later, I would regret not having called for a garnish, and, later still, I would realize that I'd failed to include the word *boneless* when I called for skinless chicken thighs.

The chicken dish was good, but it felt like an afterthought. My money was firmly on Salsa Seafood Creole and maybe the cardamom dropped muffins. Nevertheless, I licked a stamp and sent the recipe on its way. Then I took what to me is the only rational step after entering a contest. Anything else would seem like setting myself up for disappointment. I put the entire effort out of my mind.

NO proof of purchase is required to enter the Bake-Off. No secret handshake. People may enter as often as they wish. Some do. I had my five recipes; others sent in as many as two dozen.

Pillsbury won't say how many entries come in for a given contest, only that it's "tens of thousands." One contest aficionado I spoke with put his estimate at a quarter million, although he failed to substantiate this, so the number remains a mystery. But it's big.

Entries do not go directly to Pillsbury. An independent contest agency receives them, strips each entry of name and address, and identifies it by a code number. The agency winnows out incomplete entries and those that fail to qualify for some other reason. Someone connected with the beef contest I'd been in had told me that, over and over, a surprising number of people forget to include critical details: their address, the number of servings, some key ingredient, a critical step such as turning on the oven. Or they make mistakes, like writing 1 cup when they mean 1 teaspoon.

Recipes still in the running go from the agency to Pillsbury, where their home economists dig in and go to work. They sort through and select the best-looking entries, eliminating those that appear to be inaccurate, or too involved, or that call for unusual equipment and/or ingredients.

Pillsbury's team chooses about a thousand recipes to prepare and evaluate in taste tests. The recipes that pass are then scheduled for "tolerance testing" with an emphasis on consistent results under a variety of circumstances. Heaven knows they wouldn't want to end up promoting a recipe that worked only at sea level or only on a summer day or not under a full moon (altitude is in fact a very real issue). Next, they edit the recipes to conform to the company's style. They might reword a title here and there; they rearrange some of the cooking instructions, the order of things. These changes do not affect a recipe's chances. Again, home economists cook up the recipes to verify that their edited instructions are clear.

While kitchen testing is underway, yet another team of home economists checks originality against their library of more than five thousand cookbooks to eliminate any recipes that appear to be "borrowed" from existing sources. I'd love to know how they accomplish this; I can't imagine it's a task that lends itself to automation.

The winnowing process takes months. Only after the stack is narrowed down to a hundred recipes (plus a few backups, I imagine) does the independent agency reveal the entrants' names.

A new step was added to the judging process in 1998, one that took place behind the scenes. Before any cook learned that she or he would be taking command at one of the hundred Bake-Off stoves to be set up especially for the event, surveyors filtered into shopping malls across the country. I believe these were plain-clothes workers with unmarked pages of recipes on clipboards. They asked people to evaluate the written recipes on paper and rate them for general appeal and ease of preparation. From this survey, each of the hundred recipes was given some kind of consumer score that eventually was factored into the final judging, details of which were not divulged.

Pillsbury notifies finalists by phone and, as I understand it, they don't have any truck with voice mail. If necessary, their representatives keep trying someone's number until they score a direct hit. To some extent anyone receiving a call has won already, since each of them will be awarded an expense-paid trip to the Bake-Off and will be put up for the entire event. It's a three-day party.

THE call notifying me that I had been selected as a finalist came one evening in early December. Carl was out somewhere and I don't remember what I was doing when the phone rang—something in our bedroom, but I rarely took calls in there, in case I had to write down someone's number or message. I remember standing at my desk in the adjacent room. I stood for the duration of the conversation, looking out at the night through the window above my computer screen. The caller identified herself as being with Pillsbury's public relations firm. This should have tipped me off. But it didn't. I hadn't thought about how the company might notify finalists. I hadn't been paying attention. Since mailing my entries I'd been to Australia and back; Karen had a wedding to plan before the baby arrived; and I was late in writing my once-a-year poem for our Christmas card, which I invariably compose, design, and print in a last-minute panic. The Bake-Off was not in the forefront of my consciousness that evening.

In retrospect I can see why the caller expected that I would faint or squeal or exhibit some sort of emotional increase of my RPMs. I guess she'd already talked to others on the list, and many of those finalists—maybe most—had more or less fallen apart at the news of being selected. But I didn't know that, and I'm not one to leap up and down in front of strangers anyway. Despite having wanted to be selected for the Bake-Off, I didn't know enough to grasp the real significance when notification came. Veteran contesters are savvy to "getting the call."

The PR woman seemed downright disappointed that I took her news in stride. My recollection is that she asked more than once, "Aren't you excited?" I answered, "Well, I think it's very nice," but that didn't seem to satisfy her. "No. Really. It's great," I added. Then, "Thank you. I'm really pleased." But no amount of verbal response could have matched the Miss America tears she must have heard from others—and doubtless had come to expect.

Toward the end of the call, I asked which of my recipes had been selected. Salsa Couscous Chicken. My afterthought entry! At the time I still believed my Salsa Seafood Creole to be a much more sophisticated dish, and I felt a pang of disappointment at having it overlooked. Now I realize that sophisticated is not necessarily a good fit with Pillsbury; naturally, they want something with general appeal. Not everyone warms to eggplant. And okra? Let's just say I've learned to submit a recipe with okra only if there is going to be an okra promotion.

The contest was to be held in Orlando in late February. I had two and a half months to figure out a perspective and a strategy, if indeed a strategy was in order; the recipe itself could not be changed. Some of my attention for those two and a half intervening months, however, had been spoken for. Karen's due date happened to be the same as for the Bake-Off. Carl and I had scheduled a ski vacation. And the general routine of my life, such as it was, had its own demands. I had just sold my first short story and was trying to sell more. Being a writer had taken precedence over dreaming up recipes.

By nature I take a broad brush approach to most pursuits. Some might say I'm slapdash; others might call me a dabbler. The bottom line is that apart from my writing, on which I can spend ridiculous amounts of time, I'm not much on polishing or perfecting. I typically rough in, then move on. This allows me to cover a lot of territory but not in any depth. I had made Salsa Couscous Chicken only those two times, first in half-quantity, clean-out-the-fridge mode, and the second time at full volume as a last-minute check. Then I sent it in. After learning I'd be jetting off to Florida, I figured on practicing it a couple more times.

All the while I considered the whole adventure an absolute lark. Yes, I realized I stood a 1 percent chance of winning the grand prize, but that felt abstract, an amusing statistic. The concept of me winning a million dollars for stirring up a mess of chicken thighs was purely cerebral, a hypothetical curiosity. It was nothing I believed in. I didn't think for a minute I would win anyone's grand prize. All I wanted was the experience of going. Of watching. Of trying to figure out how the contest worked so I could enter another time in earnest.

There would be seventeen prizes in all: the million-dollar biggie, three at $10,000, twelve at $2,000, and a collection of kitchen appliances awarded for the easiest recipe to prepare. Eighty-three of us would go home empty-handed, save for the lavish experience. I set my sights on one of the $2,000 checks, an amount more comprehensible to me than the million, and enough of a prize to indicate a respectable showing.

I didn't fantasize about the possibility of big money. Carl and I weren't in debt; we didn't dream of buying boats, fast cars, racehorses, trips around the world, or bottles of hundred-year-old scotch. My idea of the quintessential shopping experience is a good yard sale. But competition for competition's sake is in my blood. A friend who sees me most often over a Scrabble board believes I'm fierce about winning. "It's less about you being greedy," she said, "than the simple fact of you wanting to do something a little bit better than someone else. It's almost as if you're competing with yourself."

And yet, that same friend asked why I'd entered the Bake-Off. Like the famous mountain climber, I'd say: Because it's there. Because no one was around to stop me; because the risks were small and the potential rewards great; because what does it hurt to try? The way I see it, entering a contest is not so different from playing Scrabble.

Why enter? *Why not?* It's worth making a stab at it, and if there's a prize involved, that serves as evidence of having "gotten it," of having outfoxed some problem, or solved some puzzle. If there's going to be judging, I want to see where I stack up. Maybe on some primitive level I'm looking for approval. I am the fifth of five children. Life was chaotic in our family. By the time I came along, my parents had turned to other interests. Maybe I haven't learned to stop seeking their acknowledgment even though their lives have both ended.

If I could get away with denying my competitive streak, I would. I don't know whether I'm driven to be the best or whether I simply fear being the worst. Either way, food is too subjective an arena to make those hard-and-fast rankings. There's no such thing as the best recipe in America. How does one measure cherry pie against garlic soup? Consequently I never suffered the anxiety of hoping for the biggest prize. Too many variables involved to know *how* to hope for it. That would be someone else's moment.

However, after the dust settled on the phone call from Pillsbury telling me I was a finalist, I let myself begin to hanker for one of the lesser prizes. Although I recognized that I'd already achieved my initial goal by being one of the hundred to be headed for Orlando, an actual award seemed potentially within reach. Anything beyond the trip itself and the opportunity to see what this famous contest was all about would be icing on the cake.

I'M not unique in seeing competition as an end in itself. Plenty of others are motivated by the raw fact of winning as much as—if not more than—being the contestant who gets to grab the cash.

I recently met Norita Solt, a legendary contest cook whose homemaking skills have won her so many blue ribbons at the Iowa State Fair they might reach to the Cordon Bleu and back if laid end to end. Norita is a pretty grandmother of nine with salt-and-pepper hair and a lingering allegiance toward the hippie movement, although she feels she was born too late to have become a bona fide flower child. I asked what motivates her to enter contests.

"Contesting is something I can do. I was never good at sports. In school, I was never chosen for anything. But this I can do."

"What about the money?"

"That's not it. I just like to win. Pure and simple. I love winning."

Norita went on to explain that she'd had allergies as a kid and therefore her parents were advised not to let her play outside. The setup was perfect for her to learn home arts; she was trusted to make dinner while her parents took advantage of cool evening hours in their garden. Between her mother's instruction and a willing aunt, Norita had two good kitchen guides.

Money means all kinds of different things to people—power, success, status, choice. It's a measure of a job well done, or at least that's how I see it. Proof of worth, evidence that one's ideas are acceptable.

That said, when the call came that December evening, telling me I'd been selected as a finalist, the million-dollar prize was far from my thoughts. My mind was on going to the party. I hoped I wouldn't fall on my face.

CHAPTER SEVEN

I was immediately aware of being on a countdown. I'd be leaving for Orlando on February twenty-first. Anything I wanted to say, think, or do as preparation for the Bake-Off would occur in the next ten weeks.

Before anything, we had Karen's wedding to put together. To be honest, this was not going to be the stuff of *Brides* magazine. That she was seven months pregnant didn't bother Carl or me, but the uncertainty of her financial future did. Add to that the fact that my second husband would be in attendance, and you have the makings of a soap opera. This guy hadn't deigned to be anywhere in my proximity for fifteen years. He had made quite a point of keeping his distance, and that had bothered me. Forget that his personality might tend toward the prickly, he had always seasoned the barbs with undeniable charm. I'd wanted to remain friends. I liked him. Later, he would cure me of that.

My first husband (and Karen's biological father) wouldn't be on the invitation list. He had been out of the picture for thirty years. The history with him is difficult. Carl adopted Karen when he came on the scene and wishes he could count her as his own from the start.

For the wedding Karen planned a small, intimate service in her living room. There would be about a dozen of us. Nothing but cake and champagne. She wanted me to make the cake. I knew what kind without asking.

The celebratory dessert in our family has been a *Cassata alla Siciliana* since before Karen can remember. My mother discovered the recipe in the Time-Life Foods of the World series when the Italian volume was published in 1968. Bear in mind that Husband #1 was of Italian descent. Following our split, my method of purging myself of his memory was to reject tomatoes and tomato products for a couple of silly, childish years. Eating pasta or anything pasta-related was also out of the question for a while. So the idea that this Italian cake could worm its way into our family's culinary repertoire speaks worlds for how luscious it is.

The recipe starts with a fresh pound cake. When I made this to honor my second husband's birthday one year, I did, in fact, bake a cake using a pound of butter, a pound of eggs, a pound of flour, and a pound of sugar because I was still trying to prove myself to him. (This was before I realized that no amount of effort either in or out of the kitchen would have accomplished said goal.) Suffice it to say I've since relaxed my standards and have made successful *Cassatas* with frozen Sara Lee pound cakes as the base and no one has freaked out or accused me of cheating.

For Karen's wedding, however, no prefab would do. I baked a double recipe of a not too buttery but very eggy buttermilk batter in my mother's old straight-sided pullman loaf pan. This I set aside for a day before sawing it into five horizontal layers. Next I made a ricotta filling with minced candied citron and orange peel, shards of bittersweet chocolate, Cointreau, heavy cream, and a light dash of sugar to go between the layers.

I've never made the frosting in accordance with Time-Life's instructions. They want *half a pound* of butter melted with three-quarters of a pound of semisweet chocolate and thinned with strong coffee. And I can't bring myself to smear half a pound of butter on any cake in my kitchen. So I adjusted the recipe to work with only four ounces.

The ricotta goes between the layers and the chocolate goes over the whole thing, and everything went into the fridge for twenty-four hours to ripen. The morning of the wedding, I garnished the platter with clusters of glossy, dark salal leaves, kumquats, and giant purple grapes. The effect was very Decemberish while not being Christmassy.

A confession: I was as anxious about how my former husband would react to the wedding cake as I was about whether the bride would be pleased with its presentation. For as touchy as things had been in my marriage to him, he has the capacity to defuse all that. He can be absolutely delightful company. He greeted me in Karen's living room with a big warm hug before launching into some good-natured joshing about me heading for the Bake-Off. "You always did like that girly, kitchen stuff," he said with a slightly challenging grin.

I held my tongue. Not a day to try to make a point with him. I wanted Karen's wedding to go smooth as silk, which it did. She was radiant, and, after the ceremony, the cake tasted as good as it looked. I took home an empty platter.

I'm amazed by how many people—that old husband among them—lump Pillsbury with Betty Crocker into a dismissible Suzy Homemaker lightweight stereotype. I suppose that because the kitchen is traditionally a woman's realm and because women have often been belittled for our roles as mothers and family tenders, we make an easy target.

Pillsbury didn't agree. They were intent on building us up. While we finalists were waiting for February twenty-first to roll around, the company began soliciting information about who the hundred of us were and what we had accomplished in life. Turns out we were book readers and world travelers, gardeners, hospital volunteers, mothers, and fathers, with 162 children among us. Seventy of us had received post–high school education. Eight held graduate degrees. Fourteen of us were men. Our ages ranged from seventeen to seventy-nine. And all of us were foodies to one extent or another.

Included in our group were the CEO of a communications equipment company; the owner of a video production company with a few Emmys to his credit; a medical technologist; a CPA married to a CPA; a retired NASA engineer; an art director at a communications firm; a female structural steel checker; a law student; a market analyst for a software company; a physician's assistant; a petroleum engineer; an archeologist; an architectural draftsperson; a broadcast engineer; a retired anesthesiologist; a systems analyst; a graduate student in theoretical chemistry at MIT; a quality control analyst; and a Star Trek fan.

Pillsbury learned these details via an exhaustive questionnaire. "What is the most memorable kitchen experience you've had?" it asked, and "When did you learn to cook?" and "Tell us about any kitchen disasters you've had" and "Name something unusual about your kitchen." I didn't know how to respond to their request to itemize my activities and hobbies. I think more in terms of projects: sewing, knitting, gardening. But I wouldn't say those interests define me. Pillsbury was essentially asking, Who is Ellie Mathews in a nutshell?

I couldn't think of a single interesting thing to write on those pages. I put off filling out the questionnaire until the last minute. To come up with answers that had any depth would have taken me hours. I wavered on whether to spend the effort, aware that whatever I wrote about myself or my kitchen would have zero effect on the judging process once I reached Orlando. In keeping with the company's own rules, the judges wouldn't know a thing about us as contestants when our food hit their table. The company was looking for promotional "color." Their PR machine was grinding. What they didn't seem to realize was that they wouldn't need any PR on me. I was going to the Bake-Off as an outsider. Nobody was going to care about what kind of pots and pans I used, since the limelight and I had no chance to intersect.

Carl and I had been invited out to dinner the day of the deadline for returning the questionnaire. I remember filling in short, bland, utilitarian statements on those pages, just enough to get me by. I sealed the envelope. We headed for our friends' house to enjoy a warm evening of conversation.

I could have given the Pillsbury questionnaire the same care and attention I'd given to Karen's cake. But I didn't. Funny, the way things turn out.

CHAPTER EIGHT

If I had imagined taking a completely fatalistic, la-di-da attitude toward the cooking extravaganza I'd gotten myself into, it wasn't to be. For starters, I knew I'd better execute my recipe a couple of times in advance of my arrival in Orlando—at least so I'd know what the stuff should look like.

I stirred up my entry a couple of times to make sure I had the technique squared away. It's not a tricky dish to prepare. It involves sautéing some garlic with a few chopped almonds, then adding the eight skinless chicken thighs. Then, add a cup of the Old El Paso Thick 'n Chunky Salsa, a little cinnamon and cumin, some honey, and a few dried currants. Let everything simmer for twenty minutes or so and, in keeping with the Moroccan seasoning, steam some couscous to soak up the flavors on the plate.

By January I had received from Pillsbury a KitchenAid hand mixer and a check for one hundred dollars, I guess to cover incidentals. In addition to the questionnaire, Pillsbury had also sent an affidavit for me to verify that the recipe for Salsa Couscous Chicken was, indeed, my own creation and that I had legal rights to it. Now the company sent a list for me to review of the cooking equipment they planned to supply for me at the Bake-Off: a certain kind of fork, a so-many-inch-long chef's knife, a such-and-such-sized bowl, a so-much-diameter frying pan, etc. Everything looked fine. At least, I was determined to say it looked fine. I didn't want to appear to be a prima donna, fussing over whether they would supply a two-tined fork or a three-tined fork with which to jab my chicken thighs when it came time to give them a flip in the pan. Given the number of people in the world who prepare their meals at ground level over an open fire, the exact size of a Pyrex bowl begins to seem insignificant. I like to think I'm adaptable. I like to think I could cook in the dark with a stick, a hollowed-out gourd, and a pile of hot rocks. I signed the list of equipment and sent it back.

Also in January, my list of ingredients arrived in the mail. This included the exact amounts and brand names of what Pillsbury planned to supply for me to make my required two batches of Salsa Couscous Chicken in addition to an optional third round that I'd be able to pass out as samples to members of the press and other contestants if I wanted. I didn't feel quite as cavalier about signing off on the ingredients as on the equipment list. Food is different from forks.

I usually buy very basic—but unadulterated—ingredients. Pillsbury wanted to buy me blanched, slivered almonds. Carl and I eat a lot of almonds. Costco supplies them in three-pound bags, dirt cheap. Or I buy them in bulk at our food co-op. Admittedly, skinless might have been an upgrade on my earthy approach, but I never use those prepared nuts from the supermarket baking section. They're expensive. Besides, they didn't feel familiar, and I was uncomfortable with the prospect of entering into foreign territory. When it comes to competitive cooking, give me the genuine article, since that's what I'm used to, and I'll wrestle those nuts into the pan without a second thought.

A phone call was in order.

Not only does Pillsbury supply all the spoons, forks, and bowls for the Bake-Off, they buy the food. In fact no contestant is allowed to contribute a thing. The time to negotiate the shopping list was now.

Judy Davisson was in charge of ingredients to be used at the Bake-Off. I felt embarrassed to bother her about something so trivial as what kind of almonds I cook with.

"You mean you want *natural* almonds? With the *skins* still on?" she said on the phone. She might as well have said, "You swim in the *nude*?" or, "You don't *flush* each time?" I felt ridiculous justifying my preference. "Don't the skins *darken* the dish?" Judy asked. How would I know? I've never used anything else. The anticipation of cooking in front of an audience was beginning to make me feel nervous enough as it was. I asked Judy to supply me with what I'm used to.

Next, we tackled the mistake I'd made on the chicken. But, again, I felt embarrassed to appear to be sweating out the details. For whatever reason, I didn't want anyone to imagine I took this thing seriously. *Forget that stupid nonchalance, your misplaced pride,* I could hear people say. *Get them to buy you whatever goddamned nuts will do the trick; a million dollars is in the balance.* But it didn't seem so to me. I wanted to go to this thing, keep to myself, take in the details, and come home with stories to tell.

When I wrote the recipe I had meant to put, "skinless, *boneless* thighs," which is what I'd used when cleaning out my freezer. In my usual sloppy haste, however, I failed to write the word *boneless.* I'd just said *skinless.* Skinless, bone-in thighs are not something generally available.

In the same phone call about the almonds, I asked whether Pillsbury would consider correcting my chicken mistake. We discussed the ramifications for quite a while before she went off into a huddle with her team. I found it hard to believe Judy didn't have more important things to attend to, but Judy seemed eminently available and completely relaxed about tending to the details. I mentally multiplied my niggling concerns by one hundred to get a picture of what she must be going through with the other finalists, some of whom *might* be prima donnas.

"Sorry," Judy said when she called me back a couple of days later. By now it was getting toward middle of January. "You'll have to stick with the recipe as you wrote it. We'll have the butcher pull the skin off your chicken, but we'll have to leave the bones in." I signed my revised list of ingredients and returned it, thinking, "Oh, well. This Bake-Off is a dry run anyway."

As it turned out I think the error I'd made worked in my favor. Once you take out the bones from chicken thighs, they lose their shape. Bone-in makes a much better presentation, and peeling the skin is definitely worth the effort, even if it does mean going in practically to your elbows to get it off.

ALSO in January, Pillsbury sent information on the festivities they had planned for us while in Orlando. Our Saturday arrival would be punctuated by a gala dinner that night, for which we were advised to pack something "nice" to wear. Tuesday morning would be the broadcast awards show. We were advised to have our best "television clothes" with us.

I'm not good at being told what to wear. Years ago I quit attending anything that involves a wardrobe directive. If the invitation to a Christmas party says, "wear something festive," I RSVP in the negative. I don't do lace or sparkles well. My idea of dressing up is to wear the patent leather Birkenstocks and not the suede ones. In general, I've had pretty good luck avoiding functions where people fear the clothes I choose won't meet their expectations.

Not that I don't think about clothes. I had already considered what to wear to this bash, but I was concentrating on the cooking aspect of the schedule. I wanted to be comfortable, but my usual jeans and turtleneck wouldn't cut it. If Pillsbury was going to fly me across the country at their expense, I'd better meet them halfway, wardrobe-wise. The Bake-Off was worth a few compromises. I felt terrifically pleased to have been selected, and I'm not a total rebel.

Traveling south in February meant shedding my Seattle woollies. I felt almost giddy at the thought of cheating winter. It wasn't going to be my first visit to that part of the world. For a couple of years, Carl and I had headed up the Seattle division of a computer manufacturer based in Orlando. I associated its flat landscape with the stories of sinkholes and alligators and walking catfish that my boss used to joke about. On one of our trips there, Carl and I balanced those images with a couple of amazing days in the Everglades, that breathtaking expanse of saw grass.

But Orlando itself was not a city with which I felt an affinity. My work there had been stressful. That and now being told how to dress for dinner, I felt a nagging resistance to expectations of how I would present myself. I felt absurdly determined not to be slotted into whatever stereotypes might be lurking around those hundred mini cooking stations. What I wore to cook in wouldn't make a hill of beans' difference to the judges since they'd never lay eyes on me. But I wanted to be comfortable, have plenty of pockets, be myself. I leaned toward something summery for the spirit of it all, even tropical looking. I considered a Hawaiian shirt, but that's the wrong ocean for Florida. I wasn't opposed to something shrimp-colored to get with the feel of the trip or a flamingo print, just for the outrageousness.

So, toward the end of January, with a bit of an attitude, I headed for the Seattle Goodwill store just off Dearborn Street, a veritable cornucopia of castoffs and bargains. I wanted to make it clear—possibly to myself more than anyone—that I wasn't the sort to knuckle under to convention or assumptions. That's when I saw the lucky shirt.

Okay, everyone. I don't believe in charms or incantations, and I hardly ever buy special clothes for a special event (I'm much too practical). Nor do I much subscribe to talismans or auras or crystals (I'm not superstitious, either). Nevertheless, that shirt and I came to an immediate understanding. We formed a three dollar and forty-nine cent relationship. I didn't even try it on. It wasn't going to matter whether it fit or flattered. The shirt and I had already bonded.

The heavy silk is cut short-sleeved and printed in an abstraction of travel postcards with vague suggestions of maps, of Greek architecture, of bridges spanning faraway rivers, of palm trees, and lush vegetation. It was like a vacation in itself. And, yes, there are splashes of flamingo pink. It was just the right amount of private flamboyance, perfect for the occasion, and not the real me by any stretch.

The thought that I might be photographed in living color while wearing that shirt was far from my mind. The thought that such a photograph would be reproduced in newspapers across the country was farther still.

IN addition to my countdown to the Bake-Off, there was another, more important, countdown going on at home: Karen's pregnancy was ticking along. We'd found out while Carl was working in Australia that she'd be having a girl. It was time to make sure Karen had everything necessary to keep that girl healthy and happy once she made her debut. Carl and I bought an antique cradle at an auction.

More than once in the weeks leading up to my departure on February twenty-first, I offered to forgo the Bake-Off if Karen wanted me to stay home. Who would have thought these two lifetime events would overlap? But she insisted that I go ahead. The delivery was going to be by natural means if at all possible, and it was something she and her husband had decided to go through privately, perhaps not even calling Carl and me before leaving for the hospital. If I stayed home from the contest, I wouldn't be part of a cheering section in the obstetrics wing anyway, since that wasn't the sort of birth experience they had in mind.

WHEN I say countdown, it's not as if I put all else aside. I didn't. I had more than two months' lead time and a life to keep up on in the meantime. But when friends dropped by or came to dinner, the Bake-Off subject seemed to creep into our conversations. Our friend Paul Gibson, an economist, spoke of the statistical value of my position: $10,000, by his calculation. I understood his reasoning, but pooh-poohed the notion of me standing a chance at the big prize. Another friend asked what I'd buy if I were to win. "A yellow diamond," I joked. I felt free to give a frivolous answer, since it was all conjecture anyway. The likelihood of having to make good on it felt truly remote. I would learn later that yellow diamonds are priced at a premium. Never having bought any jewelry to speak of, I thought the yellow ones were seconds—irregulars—something to appeal to my bargain-hunting nature. As it was, I already had two chunky diamonds from my grandmother's estate, each set in a perfectly good ring, and how many rings can any one woman wear?

In private moments Carl and I discussed the fantasy of big money. Not that we didn't feel our needs were more than met with what we had already. But there was one thing.

Our primitive forty acres in the Cascade Mountains didn't include running water for the cabin we'd built there. For ten years we'd been hauling drinking water in five-gallon jugs and pumping wash water from our creek with a noisy, gas-powered engine that intruded on the wilderness with its stinky exhaust. We made the setup work okay, but only by applying a good measure of patience. The pump system was a two-stage arrangement, first to an intermediate tank halfway up our hill, then to the main tank above the cabin for gravity feed. It took a couple of hours each time. Most Aprils, after the snow cleared, we'd find that winter had done something awful to the PVC pipes we'd laid the year before. If not winter, then bears. If not bears, then squirrels and their ever-sharp, curious teeth. But we loved the cabin and our ponderosa forest. For the most part Carl and I took pleasure in tinkering, whether with our rinky-dink plumbing or clearing our trails. As soon as the snow melted, our sandy soil began to heat up. Trillium and glacier lilies pushed through. Fixing the pipes we'd laid along the ground was as good an excuse as any to explore the wonders of spring.

Without a good water supply, though, I had to be stingy when it came to dish washing. I curbed my impulse toward elaborate cooking on the woodstove, which would have been fun in that quiet, private place with no telephone or electrical power. From time to time Carl and I had talked about coming up with a better system, but it would have felt like a big luxury. We were there only a couple of weekends a month or so.

More than once in the buildup to the Bake-Off, though, we returned to the dream of having a well drilled. If we were to become rich overnight, running water was our idea of a splurge.

BEFORE I learned I'd be going to the Bake-Off in late February, Carl and I had arranged a ski vacation in Whistler, British Columbia. I had prepaid, so I wasn't about to scrap the plan, having put two time-share promotions back-to-back to make it an inexpensive five-day trip. Our days there at the beginning of February coincided with the Nagano Winter Olympics.

It was the first year snowboarders had been allowed to compete, including Whistler's own Ross Rebagliati, who turned out to test positive for marijuana after arriving in Hokkaido. The town of Whistler went ape with banners taped to shop windows, exhibiting support for Rebagliati, regardless of what he had—or hadn't—smoked. Vancouver television stations were all over the story.

Carl and I, exhausted from skiing and happy to warm ourselves with the steady glow of a gas-log fire, settled in with the blue flicker of the television screen during the evenings.

A figure skating event came up in which one of the favored competitors had drawn the short straw (or whatever they use) on deciding who would skate first. "Aw, that's too bad," the commentator said. "You never want to go first. No matter how good your performance, the judges always have to leave some room."

This hit me between the eyes. Until I heard that broadcast, I'd had no idea that one's position in the sequence had any bearing on one's scores. Aha!

At the Bake-Off, we'd have all morning and part of the afternoon to prepare our recipes. It would be up to each of us to decide when to turn our work in. Going on the intelligence I picked up while watching the Olympics, I made a decision right there in that beige time-share unit. At the Bake-Off, I wouldn't try to go first. I wouldn't even go early. I would actively delay the submission of my entry until most of the other contestants had already submitted theirs.

On our last day in Whistler, Carl and I took a spin around the cross-country terrain with a big up-and-down loop of quiet among snow-heavy trees. By the time we clipped all eight skis into the rack on top of our car, I felt I'd had a good workout, what with that and the alpine skiing in the days before. We headed home, stopping at the Buddhist Vegetarian Restaurant in Vancouver's Chinatown, where the menu offers vegetarian "duck" and "abalone" and "chicken"—all ersatz meat made of gluten. Too weird for words. But delicious.

Not counting the dinner stop, it's a five-hour trip from Whistler to Seattle. Carl did the driving. We arrived home at about eight. My legs felt like rubber when I climbed out of the car. I attributed this to five days of skiing. Once in the house, however, standing at our phone machine and listening to messages, I had the distinct feeling something was wrong. And I was right. I took my temperature—and pushed the mercury to 102 degrees.

The Bake-Off was fifteen days away. The first seven of these I spent in bed, coughing and aching and running the thermometer up higher and higher. Then I felt better for a few days. Then I felt worse. The fever climbed back up. Three days before I was scheduled to leave for Orlando, I visited my doctor. Double pneumonia. Best not to travel, he warned.

But I was sick of being sick and was actually feeling that I was on the mend by then. My doctor said I wasn't contagious. I reasoned that there would be nothing life-threatening in making the trip and that I might as well feel miserable in some posh hotel room rather than in my own Kleenex-strewn bedroom. Armed with some very expensive pills and a bottle of prescription cough syrup, I folded that lucky shirt and packed it into my carry-on bag.

Chapter Nine

Saturday morning at last. Carl eased our car into the south-bound lanes of I-5 for the twenty-minute drive to the Seattle-Tacoma Airport.

"Seems weird to be going away without you," I said.

"You'll be back by Tuesday," he said. "Think of it as a business trip."

He had a good point. Just about the only time I've flown anywhere on my own has been for work. When I was in the software business it seems I was forever heading toward the airport.

He could have accompanied me. Pillsbury had invited finalists to include one guest each, but we would have had to pay his way into the meals and theme park attractions Pillsbury would be treating me to. Plus his airfare. The welcoming banquet alone would have been fifty bucks. Neither of us had ever shelled out that much for one meal. We also thought there might not be much for Carl to do while I was involved. We anticipated a fair amount of dead air for him in the role of observer. We decided to save our money for a time when we'd be in charge of choosing our own activities. Besides, the Bake-Off was clearly my project.

I arrived in Orlando a bit buzzed from the five-and-a-half-hour flight, slightly tanked up on codeine cough syrup, and mildly disoriented by the three-hour advance on my wristwatch. A woman from Pillsbury, dressed in blue with a red scarf at her neck, met me at the gate and whisked me off to the Renaissance Orlando Resort, where festivities were already under way. Pairs and trios of badge-wearing contestants were crisscrossing the gigantic atrium lobby.

More Pillsbury people greeted me at a registration table set up near the hotel entrance. One woman was in charge of Bake-Off souvenirs, so numerous they had been packed into individual zippered bags—like athletic bags—one for each contestant. The fabric was Pillsbury blue; they were huge and cram-jammed. The Bake-Off logo with the spoon and fork poking into the upper-case O had been silk-screened in white onto one side.

"Excited?" everyone suddenly seemed to be asking me. I didn't want to be a wet blanket, but frankly I was feeling more road weary than excited. At that point I simply wanted to get myself oriented and find my room. I was among the last to arrive, so there wasn't much opportunity to settle in. It was almost time for the banquet, although technically still the middle of the afternoon by my bio-clock.

In the quiet of my lavish room and very much wanting to follow the rules of conduct and blend in, I shook out the clothes I'd brought along in semicompliance with the company's semiformal guidelines. I took my temperature. Only one degree of fever. I stole a few minutes to plunge into the blue bag of trinkets for a quick survey. It's not unusual to collect a fair number of giveaways at a cook-off; the beef people had handed out freebies at their registration, too, but not as many. Here was a Green Giant beach towel; a cookbook; a trio of Cutco knives in a fitted case; a pancake turner; and everything Doughboy: key chain, pot holders, stuffed toy, dish towel. There was also an envelope of coupons for baking mixes, frozen vegetable combos, refrigerated pastries, cinnamon rolls, you name it. All free—my kind of coupons!

I thumbed through a large-format booklet in which Pillsbury's chairman and CEO, Paul Walsh, welcomed me (and everyone else) with his signed photograph on page 1. He looked like someone I had dated in high school, but here that seventeen-year-old was wearing a suit and tie and, as if he had been put through some automated age simulator, he looked old enough to be running a huge corporation instead of struggling to earn a B+ in Tilford Gribble's Washington State history class.

The booklet cover was printed edge to edge in Florida orange slices. Following the welcome page was an inside look at how

the "tens of thousands" of recipe entries had been received, processed, sorted, and tested. I looked hard at the full-page photograph of a woman in a turtleneck, sitting at a table engulfed in
mail. I tried to connect those thousands of envelopes to the ones
I had posted. Somewhere in those stacks were the envelopes with
my Seattle address in the upper left corner.

On the opposite page was the subhead, "Months of Testing
and Tasting." Beneath it read, "Pillsbury home economists chose
about 1,000 of the most appealing to prepare and evaluate…."
Next to that was a photograph of a woman wearing a lab coat
and using some sort of scientific equipment. I tried to imagine
a panel of strangers reading my typed page, my idea for how to
cook eight chicken thighs, measuring the ingredients as I'd written them, poking at the results, sniffing them, liking them.

The middle of the booklet contained information about all
one hundred contestants. We were listed alphabetically, geo-
graphically, and demographically. After that, each of us was
given a tidy bio, pulled from information on the questionnaires
we had filled out. Obviously someone had had to work hard to
get a full paragraph of cohesive information about me from the
minimal responses I'd given, but whoever that writer had been,
he or she did a good job. I didn't come off looking too awful.

Next to each bio was the title of the finalist's recipe and its
cooking category, but not the ingredients or details. Beside that
was a range number, keyed to a diagram of the Bake-Off floor
map that showed three double banks of cooking stations laid out
in the hotel's convention center ballroom. I would be assigned

to range 37, between Lisa Keys from Middlebury, Connecticut, who would be making Baja Shrimp Tacos, and Helen Klecka, from Sun City, Arizona, who would be making Apricot-Orange Chicken Picadillo.

Seeing people's names gave me butterflies in my stomach. Those people were as real as I was. As much as they couldn't make accurate assumptions about me, I couldn't assume anything of them, their motives for being here, or who they had at home cheering them on.

I can get insanely caught up in the statistics of things if given the opportunity. I made a quick count of the distribution of the finalists by cooking categories. I was surprised to see that the categories didn't tally out to four groups of twenty-five participants each. Mine, 30-Minute Main Dishes, had the most finalists, with thirty of us competing, while Quick Snacks and Appetizers included only eighteen people. That meant that any one of the Snack-ists stood a 5.5 percent chance at a category prize while I stood only a 3.3 percent chance in 30-Minute Mains.

I slipped into the heavy silk pants and matching shirt I'd packed for the banquet. My outfit was essentially a pair of low-impact, high-performance, minimally invasive pajamas, charcoal black with a comfy stretch waistband and enough pockets for my Kleenex supply—clothes guaranteed to meet the dress-up requirements while letting me blend into the shadows.

The banquet was set up in a gigantic ballroom on the hotel's main floor. I took the glass elevator down, landing near an aviary cupola with tropical birds flitting from perch to perch near the center of the lobby atrium. The room where we would be having dinner was abuzz with a couple hundred people already seated by the time I got there. I hesitated at the door, trying to absorb the setup. There were round tables with ten places each, the kind of tables that are too big to talk across. Choosing the right spot was critical, because once I was seated, my immediate neighbors would be my companions for the duration. Everyone was a stranger. I felt the same tension as I might have felt at a wedding banquet, not wanting to end up stuck next to the bride's aunt Gladys, who is just home from gallbladder surgery and itching to go over the details, or the groom's long-lost uncle, who speaks only inaudible German. I was also wary of taking up a seat between two groups of people already engaged in individual conversations, sandwiched by two backs and unable to bridge the social gap.

A table near the door was two-thirds full. I slipped in and lucked out. They were a gaggle of Pillsbury marketing managers. I couldn't have found a more outgoing bunch. On my right sat a woman from the Progresso Soup division. I discovered that she, like me, is nuts about exploring grocery stores when she travels. Some people head for posh restaurants to experience foreign cuisine; I make my way toward the supermarkets. They are a window into a region's economy, its geography, the regional agriculture, even package design and technology. I commented on how, in Australia, I'd found that eggs were sold at room temperature, stacked in aisle-end displays. The butter we had bought when visiting the Virgin Islands had originated in Ireland, and the oranges there came from Puerto Rico.

"Wouldn't you think they'd grow their own?" my companion said. "They have the climate and the soil."

Our conversation moved on to snorkeling stories. Hugely gracious, the woman from Progresso never once made me feel that I was keeping her from talking with her coworkers.

I'm pretty good at talking to strangers, but mostly that evening I felt jet-lagged and out of place. If there had been a chair and a TV tray set up for one in a dark corner somewhere, that would have been fine. No complaints as long as I had a view of the goings-on. That's what I'd come for. Fortunately, the servers showed up right away, providing a comfortable distraction.

The tall food craze was just making its debut in the world of culinary fashion. After a quick dip of my spoon into a ridiculously rich—but delicious—mushroom bisque *en croûte*, a salad of mixed garden greens arrived. They had been ingeniously wrapped in wonton skins, with sprigs of greenery sticking out the top in quite the architectural creation. Orange and grapefruit sections provided the structural foundation at the base. Citrus—of course! We were in *Florida*. Next came the main event, a fillet of beef with asparagus, carrots, and dauphine potatoes. And, as if that weren't enough to sustain us until breakfast, just for good measure, a fair number of perfectly sautéed, chubby shrimp lined one side of the plate. If we were still hungry after that, baskets of buttery rolls were kept full to overflowing. Wine pourers seemed to appear from nowhere to keep everyone's glass topped up.

I couldn't imagine what sort of coordination and staffing

was going on behind the scenes in the kitchen to have gotten us this far. But none of this beyond-the-limits extravagance prepared me for the dessert. All at once the room lights dimmed and an absolute army of servers appeared, bearing hundreds of plates with something on each that *glowed in the dark.*

Pillsbury's line of products included Häagen-Dazs. Slabs of mango and berry sorbet had been formed into what looked like individual multicolor layer cake wedges with chocolate icing. Big shards of white and dark chocolate had been stuck jauntily into the top. But that wasn't all. Fresh raspberries nestled on the side. *And* edible gold stars sparkled on the chocolate. *And* a rosette of flavored sweetened cream softened the effect. *And* fresh mint leaves provided just the right garnish. All this was served on a chilled glass plate set on an additional chilled glass plate with a luminescent ring glowing purple in between. I couldn't believe my eyes, but there it was at my place for me to admire and consume. I hated to see any of it go to waste, but I couldn't eat the whole thing. I made my way about halfway through the sorbet, popped the raspberries into my mouth, sampled the sweet foof of cream, swigged a bit of tea, bid my good night to the Progresso Soup people, and tottered off in the direction of the elevator with my Kleenex and my pneumonia coughs.

I would put in a quick call to Carl to assure him I'd arrived safely. After that I hoped I'd be able to fall asleep three hours before my West Coast bedtime. The next morning would be our orientation and final instructions for the contest.

I closed the door of my room behind me. The latch made a solid click that said "posh hotel." My experience with high-rise accommodations has been almost exclusively work related, whether I was presenting a paper at a technical conference, attending a computer graphics convention, or working a trade show. Mercifully, that part of my life is over. Lately though, when Carl has made site visits on his clients' expense accounts, I've tended to ride along with him when practical. This has put me in some snazzy digs up and down the West Coast, although snazzy invariably makes me feel slightly out of place. So while Carl slaves away, I cruise the Punjabi Market in Vancouver or poke around San Francisco's Chinatown rather than bask in hotel spas.

Sometimes we pay our own way on a work trip, such as to a meeting Carl attended in Washington D.C., when we stayed at an exceedingly utilitarian but wonderfully welcoming guest house. No wi-fi there. Carl and I often seek ways to escape the monotony of franchises. That guest house felt like home.

Carl also accompanied me to Philadelphia when I was researching a book about my naturalist grandfather. The documents and journals that comprise a record of his life are archived in the same manuscript library where Benjamin Franklin's papers and those of Lewis and Clark are maintained. Originals. Carl and I stayed in a creaky hotel in the historic district. The walk up to our fourth-floor room was positively aerobic and the descent practically life-threatening. No wi-fi there either.

We were delighted to be in Philadelphia. And while it may well be that Carl and I don't gravitate to five-star hotels and restaurants, it would hardly be said that we live the lackluster lives of ascetics with nothing to break the gloom of gruel and self-denial, day after gray monotonous day. In our own way we enjoy a steady stream of luxuries. Hand-rolled, single-estate tea, for example, is not out of the question. While I can barely distinguish shiraz from chardonnay, I can go into raptures about hairy crab oolong or gunpowder pinhead extra-choice, or topaz pu-erh, which is aged in caves and tastes vaguely and magnificently of dirt on the second or third pouring.

Sadly, no loose-leaf tea was to be found in the Renaissance Orlando Resort, just a bag of Lipton's dragged through a cup of almost-hot water. Except for the palm fronds clacking against themselves in the breeze outside my window, my room could have been Anywhere, USA. I felt very much alone—bravely so—as if on a mission.

I called Carl. He was spending his Saturday afternoon giving the floorboards of our second-story landing the once-over with a belt sander. "So how was the banquet?" he asked.

"Hotel food. A bit excessive by our standards, but beautifully done. You wouldn't believe the dessert. It was so elaborate I wrote down the details in my notebook. And the Pillsbury people are all nice as pie."

"What about your lungs. Feeling any better?"

"Still coughing my brains out."

"Dragamundo. I guess that's what the codeine's for."

"It'll get better," I said. "Might as well be coughing here as there and keeping you awake all night."

Carl and I can easily burn up the phone wires with interminable small talk, but I needed to get to bed on East Coast time. Winding up the conversation, he said, "Don't forget." He always says that at the end.

"I know," I said, feeling small and alone. "Me, too." Our shorthand for saying we love each other. I recradled the phone without making a sound.

I poked around in the gargantuan marble bathroom, taking inventory of the toiletries. Shampoo is a good indicator of hotel quality, starting with the no-star joints that don't give you any at all and where the hot and cold faucet handles might not even match. Then there are the places where shampoo is supplied in little foil packets impossible to open when your hands are wet. Better hotels, of course, lay out wee baskets lined with washcloths in signature folds. Hand lotion, conditioner, a second bar of soap, a sewing kit nestled in designed arrangements. The Renaissance Orlando Resort offered that and more: emery boards, cotton balls, Q-tips.

My room was quiet save for the steady respiration of the HVAC. Two beds and no one to share them with. I spread out my stuff on the one near the window. I organized the Doughboy trinkets and flipped through the contest book. I tested one of the Cutco knives on a piece of paper. Sharp. But then, most new knives are sharp.

In the elevator and halls I had seen evidence of social clumps already formed or in the process of forming. Other contestants had brought their husbands, wives, sisters, best friends. Some finalists knew each other from past cooking contests or even previous Bake-Offs.

Pillsbury itself had brought its own staff. Hosts, runners, technicians, home economists, and promoters of various sorts greeted me at every turn. Whirlpool, the Bake-Off appliance sponsor, was present in full force with its employees, too. Electricians would be installing one hundred ranges, a bank of refrigerators, microwave ovens, blenders, food processors, all things electric and with the potential of being turned on at once come Monday. KitchenAid, a division of Whirlpool, had sent a bevy of promoters. Cutco Cutlery—another official Bake-Off sponsor—had flown in a scatter of its people. And somewhere in all of this, running concurrently with the Bake-Off, a food industry marketing conference of some sort was going on in distant rooms. It was hard not to think of the money involved and how much that must add to the cost of a bag of flour or a box of cake mix once it reaches the supermarket shelf.

I brushed my teeth and slipped into my PJs in what was to be my home away from home for that night and two more. This bedtime, perhaps the most strange, a Saturday night alone. Sunday we'd have our orientation. We'd cook on Monday. Then, Tuesday, we'd all go home.

Chapter Ten

Between Pillsbury's marketing convention, the contest participants, its judges, the sponsors, and associated support staff, we took up a goodly number of Marriott's 778 rooms for that extended weekend. One of them, I already knew, was occupied by a man I was eager to see.

Starting with Eleanor Roosevelt in 1949 at the first Bake-Off and followed by the Duke and Duchess of Windsor, Bess Truman, Mamie Eisenhower, Pat Nixon, Abigail Van Buren, and Ronald Reagan, Pillsbury has made a point of including noteworthy guests. Art Linkletter hosted the awards show for many years. More recently, the company has hired a variety of "television personalities" to add to the dazzle. Of all the possible singers, dancers, and entertainers they could have come up with the year I participated, they couldn't have hit on a better one for me than Alex Trebek.

If my mother and father were alive, I'm sure they'd love for me to say I watch nothing more than *60 Minutes* and *Nova* on television. Better yet, they'd have me declare that I'm so highly evolved intellectually that I don't own a television. In fact, between our condominium in Seattle and where we now live on the Olympic Peninsula, Carl and I own four. I've even been known to indulge in an occasional *Jeopardy!* broadcast. The appeal must go with my mania for quizzes.

As the host of *Jeopardy!* Alex Trebek lends dignity to the world of game shows. When I learned he would be the star of "my" Bake-Off, I felt giddy at the thought of seeing him in person, of maybe even meeting him. On air, he presents himself as an exceedingly gracious and well-informed host. His pronunciation of people's names and of foreign words, for example, is careful and accurate. *Jeopardy!* may be just one more televised quiz show, but it's one in which no one is made to look foolish. No one has to wear a silly hat or howl like a coyote. Alex acts like a grown-up.

Sixteen hours into my Bake-Off experience, there he was on Sunday morning, in blue jeans. Breakfast was a sit-down-and-be-served affair. Alex was slathering jam on his toast along with the rest of us. Seeing him across the muffle of white tablecloths and big, starched napkins, I thought he seemed as gracious in person as on the air.

I had only ever seen the man in a suit and tie, standing eight inches high, at most, on my Sony screen. Viewing Trebek at full, flesh-and-blood scale and in casual clothes felt surprisingly intimate. After most of our eggs and bacon had been dealt with and plates whisked away, a few people asked for his autograph.

My experience meeting "known" people is limited. When I was twenty-five I attended a party in Menlo Park, California, along with the novelist Ken Kesey. I had read both *Sometimes a Great Notion* and *One Flew Over the Cuckoo's Nest* the previous summer, while my then husband finished up a postdoctoral fellowship on Cape Cod, and while I was feeling especially homesick for the Northwest. In addition to being a dynamite storyteller, Kesey had been masterful at capturing the atmosphere I'd grown up knowing. I was ga-ga to meet the man. In person, as on the page, he came across as magnetic and energizing and enormous.

In a juvenile effort to show how cool and with it and hip I could be, I made a mess of it when introduced. I'm sure whatever I said to Kesey made no sense to him whatsoever.

The social gradient between persons known and unknown is a steep one to navigate. We, the public, feel acquainted with celebrities ahead of time; they know nothing of us. And there's not enough of any one of them to go around when the many of us want to get cozy or sidle up to them. The laws of supply and demand apply.

Much as I would have liked to have a reason to chat up Alex Trebek right then and there at breakfast, I couldn't think of a single thing to say to him or ask of him that hadn't likely been said or asked by a thousand fans before me. Approaching him would have felt to me as if I were imposing on him.

A few years ago Carl and I had occasion to entertain an Oscar-winning Movie Star at our house for dinner. In many ways, except for the Famous Face among us with its Big White Teeth, it was an ordinary evening among pleasant but ordinary people. The father of a friend of ours, he was visiting from Los Angeles and brought with him his third-wife-to-be and her sister, who happened to live in Seattle. The connection was that this Movie Star father and his sweetie had both attended the George School, a Quaker institution. I invariably jump at the chance to meet my friends' family members, be they ditchdiggers or Nobel laureates. It helps fill in the gaps in my understanding of someone's history and tales.

I was reminded of the time, years earlier, when a friend of my parents became the president of Radcliffe College. Part of her employment package included a gigantic house to occupy and a cook to take command of the kitchen for official college functions. The story goes that the cook freaked out when she saw Julia Child's name on a guest list for lunch one day. What cook wouldn't?

I've thought about that predicament and I know what I'd do: go as far away from French cooking as I could possibly get, a Japanese peasant meal, for example. If I can't join someone at their own game, I'll try playing a game where they might not know the rules.

I coached myself ahead of time to treat my friend's famous father as I would treat any guest: welcome him at the front door, invite him in, and do my best to make him comfortable at our table. I served cabbage rolls with steamed buttered beets. For dessert I made a toasted almond and ricotta sorbet. I wasn't about to compete with the Movie Star's high-end world. Later on I would describe the evening as the night a Movie Star came to dinner. Later still, I laughed when I learned that this major Hollywood actor referred to the same evening as when he had had dinner with some "regular people." But the evening had gone well. He and I had something in common: we both treasured his daughter.

Alex Trebek and I had no such social glue. I hung back amid the tink of people stirring their second cups of coffee. Too reserved to approach Trebek for an autograph or any other contrived purpose, I could only hope he would seek me out later as one of his assigned contestants to interview.

Immediately following breakfast, we were hustled into the adjoining room, where one hundred chairs had been set up in orderly rows. The Pillsbury people had organized what seemed a constant configuration and reconfiguration of one grand room after another, all opening onto a lobby with a red carpet and elaborate Italian Renaissance architectural detailing.

This Sunday morning orientation session was our only chance to get the nitty-gritty of what to expect, what would be permitted come Monday when we would finally get down to the cooking aspect of all this revelry. No guests or outsiders were allowed to listen in on this final review of the rules.

When an official Pillsbury representative stepped to the front of the room, we all grew quiet.

Karen Couné was as friendly and efficient as all the other Pillsbury people had been. She was attractive and well put together. She spoke with the elusive flat vowels of a midwest accent that I can never imitate. She delivered a concise overview of what to anticipate once we tied on our blue aprons.

We were assigned to ranges by number. I remembered mine was 37. Each cooking station, Karen told us, would consist of a thirty-six-inch cabinet and countertop and a four-burner electric range. No sinks; no running water. If we needed water, a runner would fetch it for us. The ratio of runners to contestants was one to four. Runners would fetch us our refrigerated ingredients as needed. Monitors would be available for questions. Technicians would be on-site for help in operating the ranges. Not everyone was familiar with their digital controls. The utensils we'd all signed off on weeks ago would be stocked in our cabinets, our so-many-inch-long knives, our thus-and-so-diameter frying pans.

"When you think you're ready to send your dish in to the display table, let your runner know," Karen explained. "He or she will escort you and your dish to the contestant photo area, where you'll need to have your picture taken before you submit your dish. When you have your entry ready for the judges, a runner will accompany you and carry your dish to the door, where you will sign a statement and turn in the dish."

Karen went on to outline the order of things for the rest of our stay: theme-park entertainment and an elaborate dinner for the remainder of Sunday. Cooking on Monday until midafternoon, followed by a blowout party at Universal Studios Monday night. Then, on Tuesday, the nationally televised awards show. Immediately following the announcement of the prizes, we'd all depart for the airport and the Bake-Off would be over.

Save for the million-dollar grand prize winner. Marlene Johnson was introduced to explain how that person would be flown to Los Angeles for a guest appearance on *The Rosie O'Donnell Show* on Wednesday. People around me stirred with excitement at this surprise. I thought Marlene had said "Rosy O'Donald," but whatever the name, I was clueless. A giddiness surrounded me. Judging from the reaction by other contestants, the L.A. thing sounded like a side trip the winner would enjoy.

The winner from the previous Bake-Off had been given a guest spot on *The Tonight Show with Jay Leno*, a show I watch. *That* was something I knew enough about to get excited.

In our registration packets, we'd all been given oversized luggage tags printed in Pillsbury red, white, and blue. Marlene instructed us to fill these out and attach them to our bags before assembling them in the hotel lobby and entering yet another gigantic ballroom for the awards show. One last time we would be grouped by range number and cooking category. This would facilitate the television camera crews' ability to match names and faces.

While we were all tucked up with the awards ceremony, Marlene continued, someone from Pillsbury would tiptoe around the cordoned-off luggage and identify the bag belonging to the million-dollar winner. They would pull it from the stack and route it for the trip to Los Angeles. A nervous titter swept across the contestant orientation at the description of this undercover stealth. I wondered which of the men and women around me would be flying to L.A. I didn't know what the O'Donald television show was; I didn't know who the winner would be, but whoever it was going to be, more power to them if they thought it sounded like fun.

I felt glad no one except a bus driver would have to deal with my little black carry-on bag. The piece was on its last legs, with ripped piping and an iffy zipper. I had better bags, but I'd intentionally packed light to avoid checking luggage.

A few more Pillsbury people stepped to the front to go over details. The Cutco knives would be ultrasharp; be careful. A first-aid station would be set up, stocked with plenty of Band-Aids to cover cuts and burns. Cuts of a certain severity would require working with rubber gloves.

Contestants would be able to enter and leave the room as they wished, but we weren't allowed to take anything into the cooking area with us; no bottles of soda, no cups of coffee, nothing to eat. We were to wear our blue aprons and our red-white-and-blue ribbon name badges. The media would be held behind a cordon for the first thirty minutes while we got comfortable with our kitchens. After that, we could expect to see members of the press wandering around, watching us. We were encouraged to answer their questions, but if they approached us during a critical step in preparing our recipes, we should feel free to keep them at bay. And, finally, each of us was required to complete a short video interview at some point while we were cooking; the crew would find us. Alex Trebek would be conducting brief interviews as well.

The orientation was turned over to questions. What's to ask? I thought. Our ingredients and equipment would be provided; our recipes couldn't be altered. End of story.

I'm a fatalist.

Others, however, weren't so cavalier. One woman wondered what to do if her oven didn't heat up. Someone else asked, "What if my cake falls?" Someone's recipe had an intermediate step that required chilling; where would the fridges be? "What if I drop one of my eggs?" one woman asked. She wondered whether it would be replaced. No. It wouldn't.

With each answer came the subtle reminder: This is a *contest*. Common sense and care are part of the competition. Burn your cookies and *you won't win*.

CHAPTER ELEVEN

Because I had set my sights low for my outcome in the Bake-Off, I didn't feel especially nervous at the prospect of stirring a few simple ingredients into a pan come Monday morning. It wasn't as if I didn't have a perfectly good set of written instructions: the recipe I'd submitted from the comfort of my own kitchen months prior. Maybe it was pride, maybe bravado, but I'd reached the point of not worrying about preparing my thirty-minute "quick and easy" dinner. If I blew it, what would be the loss? I'd still go home having experienced the biggest recipe contest America has ever known.

What did throw me a little was the thought of being on good behavior with a bunch of strangers for three days running. I had no one to relax with.

Many of the questions at our orientation session seemed the direct product of people's anxiety. I may be neurotically oriented to a roll-with-the-punches attitude. I kept wanting to stand up and say something soothing like, "We really all need to cast our fates to the wind at this point, don't we? Doing our best while trying to make this be fun. Remember, we know how to cook; that's what got us here." But the questions continued. Someone implied that her recipe was special; someone else suggested she had special techniques and special requirements. People were worried about things that I didn't think needed to be worried about: "What if the power fails?" "What if I trip and break my arm?" The Q&A went on and on. Two men to my right started openly mocking the questioners in unmodulated whispers.

The men quickly drifted to another subject. It might have been duck hunting. Whatever their topic, their voices were distracting and, I thought, terribly rude both to Pillsbury and to all of us seated. Obviously, some of the contestants were in a frazzle. What did it hurt us to give them their moment? I shot the men a look. No effect. They kept on talking. Have some courtesy, I thought. I shot them another look. Still talking, no longer bothering to keep their voices low. I felt sorry for the speaker, soldiering on with patience. I felt embarrassed to be witnessing such disrespect.

Finally, I blurted to these men, "Maybe you could have your conversation later?" I shouldn't have waited for a head of steam to build up, because I'm sure by the time I spoke I sounded demanding and bitchy. The men gave me a sour look, but they shut up. Victory. But my heart was thumping. I'm no good with confrontation.

As a guest of the company, I felt protective of Pillsbury and the party they were throwing for us. Our next activity was going to be an afternoon at Walt Disney World, lunch included, all at Pillsbury's expense. The least we could do was sit quietly for a few more minutes.

We had the option of visiting either the Magic Kingdom or Epcot. After that Sunday morning orientation, buses would arrive at the hotel to take us to either of the Disney attractions for the afternoon. Buses would again materialize at the theme parks late in the afternoon and deliver us to Planet Hollywood for dinner that night.

I had been to Disney World a couple of times. It's a guilty pleasure, the entertainment equivalent of a high-fructose, low-fiber snack. In terms of making the choice of where to go, I couldn't imagine experiencing the Magic Kingdom solo. Who wants to ride up Space Mountain without a giggle partner? It would have just felt too hollow. I've never even gone to the movies alone.

As the orientation meeting broke up, contestants began making tentative arrangements to sit together on the ten-minute bus ride, to pal around together at the theme parks. A few people asked if I'd like to join them. I didn't want to hurt their feelings, but I declined. Up until a few days ago I'd been sick in bed; I was still feeling wobbly around the edges and I didn't want to slow anyone down.

Neither did I want anyone slowing me down by having

to linger at an exhibit or a trinket stand I wasn't interested in. Sometimes the pleasure of privacy is all about pace. I wanted to reserve the option of bailing out on an attraction when bailing out was called for. Maybe I'd like to sit on a bench in the Florida sun and do nothing more strenuous than watch people drift by.

Carl and I had visited Epcot shortly after it opened in 1982, when we had some extra time on a work trip. I especially remembered the leapfrog fountains. As far as I was concerned, those whimsical waterworks could count as valid entertainment for a good part of my Pillsbury afternoon, me watching ropes of water chase each other through the air, into the ground, and back into the air again. I didn't feel compelled to wring every last ounce out of what Epcot had to offer. My goal for the day was to have plenty of what I call "float time," when I don't have to answer to anyone, *respond* to anyone. I wanted to relax into my own thoughts and daydreams, accomplishing nothing tangible but everything grounding. I wanted the afternoon off, to excuse myself from the Bake-Off and all the social electricity that went with it. Epcot and the passivity of being its audience was the answer. So easy to slip into. So wonderfully anonymous.

My recollection of Epcot's indoor attractions, from being there with Carl, was of one plushy theater after another, where highly produced short subjects smacked of tourist-board propaganda. Projected at a CircleVision/IMAX/multimedia level of sensory exhaustion, those movies might be thrilling in their ability to grab me by the cinematic throat for their twelve or fifteen minutes duration, but I didn't feel compelled to see each one. How many helicopter shots of snowy ridges and sweeping wheat fields can one person absorb?

I had briefly considered skipping the Epcot experience altogether and staying in my hotel room with my coughs and my bottle of guaifenesin with codeine. I didn't know to what extent three rounds of cooking my chicken thighs under scrutiny would tax my stamina come Monday. I didn't want to undermine myself by overdoing things on Sunday. But staying at the hotel would have meant missing out on a free lunch and the dinner Pillsbury had planned. It would have left me stranded in a land of parking lots and highway interchanges as far as the eye could see, a land of dazzling flat lawns bigger than the town where I grew up. I'd have been at the mercy of Marriott's chefs with not so much as a hot dog stand within walking distance.

We had half an hour to kill before the buses would leave. In my room I tucked the thermometer under my tongue for a full two minutes. Normal. I took a deep breath and gathered a handbag of what I thought I'd need for the afternoon.

One of the Bake-Off hosts, with her pretty hair and inviting smile, stood at the door of the chartered bus I waited to board. Clouds boiled up on the horizon and the weather looked iffy. Along with tickets to the Disney attractions, she was passing out disposable plastic rain parkas in case the skies opened up. She also handed out envelopes of Disney dollars. Twenty-five bucks apiece for lunch to spend as we wished.

Boarding the bus solo took me back to my grade-school

days, that all too familiar schoolgirl awkwardness of choosing a place to sit while others chattered in pairs. I filed to the back. A few people put their hands palm down on empty seats, indicating that those were being saved for someone else. No matter. It had been my choice to go it alone.

EPCOT'S parking lot was a herringbone pattern of vacationers' automobiles. One hundred and forty-four concrete acres, I learned later. Peering through the bus's tinted window at what must have been thousands of cars, I wondered how often on an average day people forgot where they had left theirs. Or locked their keys in. Or returned to flat tires following an afternoon's revelry in all things Disney. For all I knew, Mickey & Co. had an entire team assigned to parking lot snafus. We passed a gray Honda like my daughter's and I wondered how often gray Hondas got mixed up, someone from Ohio trying to drive away in one with Iowa plates where the key had mysteriously fit in the door lock.

But I didn't have to worry about any of that. Our chartered bus delivered us right to Epcot's front gate.

Epcot is an acronym for Experimental Prototype Community of Tomorrow. Walt Disney himself dreamed up the concept, but died before its completion. People say that by the time it was all slicked up and ready for business in 1982, it probably didn't much resemble what he envisioned, but the idea was, more or less, to expose visitors to the cultures of the world with a little education thrown in. The place resembles a world's fair more than an amusement park. It's arranged in two distinct nodes: first, the quasi-scientific zone around the Innoventions exhibit, where physics, biology, and space travel dominate. And second, the World Showcase, where eleven countries' pavilions encircle the manicured shoreline of a forty-acre lagoon in supposed representation of the myriad ways humans live on the Earth. Cuisine, history, architecture, and shopping are evident themes. The idea, I think, is to represent the full range of the world's customs and aesthetics in a nifty three-hundred-acre microcosm and its 1.2-mile intercontinental paved walk. Russia, Spain, the Middle East, and most of the African nations declined to sponsor installations, however, resulting in a strangely skewed, Northern-hemisphere, tourist-eye view of the world.

I was struck by the brightness of the place. Apparently, prior to construction, Kodak had gotten together with Disney on what color to tint the concrete walkways. They're pink. That makes the grass look greener than it really is. I'm told it also makes photographs look brighter. I hadn't taken a camera with me to Florida. Without seeing the place represented on film, however, the colored sidewalks gave me a heightened sense of artificial cleanliness.

From time to time in my aimless stroll around the World Showcase Lagoon, I subtracted three hours from my watch to imagine Carl and what he might be doing within our gray-green Seattle walls. Babies in strollers had me thinking of Karen approaching the end of her pregnancy and I instinctively crossed the fingers of my right hand inside my pocket, not wanting to think about the risks of delivery. I saw a man who looked like my former boss and I thought of the company I'd worked for not forty miles from where I stood. I wondered what had become of the people involved there.

It was an afternoon adrift, one that felt mildly surreal. I sometimes imagine myself as if seen from an airplane. I couldn't help but marvel at the combination of forces that had landed me in this flat and foreign place so far from home. I tried to connect Florida to my corner of the country, with its Northwest mountains and forceful rivers of glacial meltwater. Years before, in one of my geography courses at the University of Washington, we'd been shown a documentary film called *The Powers of Ten*, in which the universe is pictured at different scales of magnification, starting with an overhead shot of a picnic by the shores of Lake Michigan, then zeroing in on the back of one of the picnicker's hands, then the cells in his skin, then the DNA within the cells, and so forth down to the atomic particles. It takes only a few steps to reach a profound level of abstraction.

Meanwhile, by midafternoon my hunger was no abstraction. It was a cinch I wouldn't be indulging myself in any twenty-five-dollar lunch. A few people had recommended various eating opportunities. "Go to the Japan pavilion," one had said. "Their tempura is melt-in-your-mouth." That's what I was afraid of. Too much grease. One of the reasons Carl and I rarely eat out is that restaurants are so apt to give you too much of a good thing—oil, butter, cream, salt, sugar, garlic, you name it. But when we do select a restaurant, it's invariably something authentically ethnic. We love food from Korea, Vietnam, Malaysia, Thailand, Laos, Singapore, India. I looked at the menu in front of the China pavilion's Nine Dragons and had the feeling that Epcot's execution of "crispy chicken stir-fried in a spicy brown sauce" would have been heavily translated from Mandarin into English.

So I took a functional approach, snacking at sidewalk level as I moseyed along through my private afternoon. Can we call popcorn and an ice cream bar a balanced meal if popcorn counts as a whole grain and ice cream counts as a dairy serving?

I left Epcot feeling totally relaxed. The skies had cleared. Pillsbury's emergency raincoat stayed comfortably folded in my handbag. My decision to indulge in what Epcot had to offer had been just what the doctor ordered.

Leaving the theme park behind, I found my way outside the gate to wait for the bus. A few by-now familiar Bake-Off faces trickled out from the crowd. It felt good to regroup and compare notes. In body and spirit, I was ready for whatever the evening might bring.

CHAPTER TWELVE

A couple minutes' drive from Epcot, Pillsbury hopefuls poured out of buses onto Planet Hollywood's pavement and queued up under a tongue of awning that extended from a big blue sphere of a building. We numbered about a hundred and fifty, including finalists and their guests. One might think a group the size of ours would overtake any restaurant, but Planet Hollywood was huge. At three stories, it's the biggest link in that chain of eateries. And possibly the loudest.

We sat at a continuous table that snaked around the mezzanine level overlooking an alarming clutter of movie star pictures and entertainment paraphernalia hanging from the walls and ceiling. An intact Volkswagen Beetle that had been used in a Disney film dangled ominously from some sort of rigging. I wondered about petroleum products dripping onto salads at the lower level. Would unsuspecting diners know the difference between Thousand Island and transmission oil among their lettuce leaves in that dim light?

Our meal began with colorful layered drinks in curvaceous, footed glasses. The rainbow of liquids had been poured in the manner of a *pousse-café* but without the alcohol of real liqueurs. These sweet drinks, with their cellophane straws and their maraschino cherries, caused a stir, although it was difficult to hear exactly what people were saying about them, since the background music in the place was very much in the foreground. Earsplitting, in fact. Did I mention it was loud? Beyond a three-foot radius communication was largely by gesture.

Platters arrived, heaped with what looked like skinny egg rolls. I picked up one of the custom-printed menus that had been placed along the center of the table to see what I was about to eat. It said, "Appetizer: Thai Sticks." How bizarre, I thought. I looked around to see whether anyone else had taken notice of what these fried bits on the platters were called.

I hope you'll forgive me for knowing this, but in some circles, a Thai stick refers to a quantity of extremely resinous cannabis buds bound with a length of fine silk thread to a slender piece of bamboo. I can still picture my friend's manicured hands unwinding one of these arrangements over a sheet of Zig-Zag rolling paper. Is it possible no one connected with Planet Hollywood—or the entertainment world—or my fellow diners—was aware of this gaffe in terminology? Was it only me?

I don't usually go around bragging about my slim familiarity with recreational drugs, but it would have felt false for me to overlook this bizarre choice of terms without doing some sort of reality check. I turned to my immediate tablemates.

"Does anyone find this a bit strange?" I said, positioning my finger under the line in question while facing the menu outward for others to read. I felt as if I were about to utter an obscenity at a church picnic while watching to see whether anyone would flinch.

"No. Why?" they said.

"Well, that used to be a reference to astonishingly high-end marijuana," I said. "It's a little like promoting sugared doughnuts by saying they're sprinkled with angel dust." Blank stares. "You just wouldn't do it, is all." More blank stares. "This is a family restaurant," I said finally.

Either none of the midwesterners in my midst was hip to drug slang or they couldn't hear what I was saying over the deafening thud-thud-thud of the music. Maybe no one could bring herself to admit to ever having taken a toke. Then the woman across and to the right reached for a copy of our menu page. She gave me a knowing look. Who would think I'd make a connection with someone at a function as squeaky clean as the Pillsbury Bake-Off over my rusty history with controlled substances? But that's what kicked off my acquaintance with Penny Nichols.

A full day into the Bake-Off and we'd had our get-acquainted banquet, our breakfast with Alex Trebek, our orientation meeting, a trip to Disney World, two bus rides, and now the full-course treatment at Planet Hollywood. Yet I was still stuck in the *Where are you from? What's your recipe?* and *Is this your first Bake-Off?* level of socializing with most of the other contestants. Add to that the optional fourth question: Are you excited? (or the more demanding form, *Aren't* you excited?) and my face hurt from smiling.

Penny and I zipped right past the fact that she lived in Baton Rouge and had come to the Bake-Off via her recipe for Asparagus with Sweet Pepper–Walnut Sauce. I learned she was an architectural drafter/AutoCAD specialist at Louisiana State University and that she was the single mother of a fourteen-year-old girl. I learned she had verve. She and her daughter had spent two weeks camping in the wilds of Alaska.

We sat together on the bus ride back to the hotel.

Finally, I *was* fired up to the level expected of me—not about cooking or contests but about forging a possible friendship. I was barely aware of the pneumonia diagnosis I'd received only five days prior. I felt terrific.

And speaking of health, as our motor coach ground its way into the night, word sizzled up and down the aisle that the most elderly contestant among us had been carried off to the hospital during the middle of our dinner. Maybe it was the too loud music. Early in the evening I had screwed up my courage to ask our server whether the volume couldn't be adjusted to a level compatible with human endurance.

"I know," the server shouted back over the din. "I get asked to do that all the time."

"Well?" I said.

"But we can't change it." He looked cute and sweet and young in his helplessness. I wondered what the decibels would do to the man's cochleas, night after deafening night. Did he mean it was physically impossible, as in no access to the volume control, or did he mean he and other servers were simply not allowed to touch it?

The sticky glass from my rainbow drink had been whisked away at the end of the meal with an offer to bring me a clean one just like it to keep as a souvenir of the evening. But what would I do with one oddball glass after struggling it home—put a goldfish in it, maybe?

I was tired. It had been a long day. The quiet of my room felt good. Earlier, at our orientation meeting, Karen Couné had asked us to have our blue aprons with us when we showed up for breakfast Monday morning. George and Sally Pillsbury, grandparents of the Bake-Off and whose names really are George and Sally, were scheduled to lead us in a grand march from our bacon and eggs into the giant room full of tiny kitchens where we'd be spending the most intense part of our day.

I tried on my apron over the jeans I'd been wearing and assessed the overall effect in Marriott's full-length mirror, trying to decide whether knotting the apron loosely in back was more flattering than bringing the ties around to the front. Better in front. I loaded one pocket with a supply of Kleenex, another with Chapstick. I removed the apron, folded it neatly, and laid it on the spare bed so I'd be sure to remember it in the morning. I laid out the silk shirt I'd bought at the Seattle Goodwill. I smoothed suitcase wrinkles out of my cotton pants—sage green—and laid them next to the shirt. Time for bed. I took a slug of cough syrup. After my head touched the pillow, I didn't know where I was or who I was until the digital beep-beep-beep of early morning brought the Florida sun leaking around the edges of heavy hotel drapes.

Showtime.

CHAPTER THIRTEEN

At breakfast Monday morning, Alex Trebek sat at a long VIP table with his two little kids and his gorgeous wife. He was wearing charcoal slacks, a gray polo shirt, and a black cardigan, a golf sweater with big, loose sleeves. All very natty. Next to their foursome sat a couple who looked to be in their mid seventies, whom I assumed were George and Sally Pillsbury. He is the great-grandson of the company's founder. Word has it that he, fresh out of Yale, attended the very first Bake-Off in 1949 and had been attending ever since. Half a century later, it appeared the man was still going strong although he had long since retired from work at the flour mill and its associated divisions.

I was impressed to see the Pillsburys sporting Bake-Off name badges just like the rest of us—as if they needed official identification for entrance to the cooking arena. Without a doubt George and Sally were comfortable in the role of gracious hosts, bright eyed and fully decked out, he in a gray suit and she in the clearest sky blue gabardine imaginable and with plenty of tasty-looking jewelry to go along. They both appeared spry and at the same time vaguely regal: the king and queen of our event. I imagined they'd had a nice life together.

With the crumbs of our buffet breakfast cleared away, the Bake-Off project director introduced the Pillsburys, who stood and told us how happy they were to be there with us, America's best home cooks. Next, we received a few last-minute instructions. We were to queue up two by two, following the regal couple into the hotel's reception foyer and then into the grand ballroom, where our kitchens had been set up.

I refolded my starched linen napkin, laid it beside my plate, and retrieved my blue apron from where I'd stashed it under my chair. I rose to my feet and tied it on. Others were doing the same. A crackle of excitement skittered around the room. By now, enough random conversations had made it clear that a good number of my fellow contestants had their sights set on winning the big prize. The make-or-break moment approached.

To add to the stir, a living edition of the company's mascot—the Pillsbury Doughboy—came lumbering into view at the door in all his eight-foot, white splendor. A good two feet of his height was hat and head, his face wider than it was tall and with a permanent smile stitched on. Following the Doughboy came the Little Sprout, a cartoonlike version of the Green Giant. The

Sprout was not quite as tall as the Doughboy, but equally ample around the middle, slightly more agile, and dressed in green on green. Unlike the Doughboy, the Sprout had fingers and toes. In fact, the Doughboy had no feet. Not even a suggestion of heels or ankles. Just the termination of his chubby cylindrical legs on flat, white discs the approximate diameter of a human foot. They looked a bit like an elephant's flat, round feet, except an elephant's feet at least have toenails.

Towering over George and Sally, the mascots led our parade. A blast of disco music fired up over the hotel's sound system. The Bake-Off people wanted us to march in formation and whoop it up while the media and assorted onlookers looked on. The problem is that whooping it up doesn't come easily to me at nine in the morning. Neither does marching around to piped music.

None of my weddings had me proceeding down an aisle in a fluffy dress. I was in a parade a long time ago. But as soon as the Chrysler I rode in lurched into gear and rolled down State Street in Olympia, Washington, I knew I wasn't cut out for waving to the crowd from a convertible. I've joined in probably no more than two conga lines in my entire life and I think alcohol was a deciding factor in each case. I am not an eager performer, to say the least.

The more I saw people around me clapping time to the thumpy music and bumping hips with each other and high-fiving left and right, the more I wanted to crawl under the nearest stove. I hoped I wasn't disappointing anyone with my inhibitions. I have never high-fived anyone in my life, let alone someone in a Pillsbury Doughboy suit. I sought the security and privacy of range 37.

To say that the room arranged for cooking was enormous doesn't really capture its gigantic scale. Some people think in terms of football fields; I lean more toward Costco stores as a comparative metric unit. This was about half of Seattle's flagship installation. Three double banks of stoves stretched from the entrance to the far corner, where a couple dozen refrigerators stood at attention, their white doors identified with range numbers. Contestants wouldn't be allowed to fetch their own perishables. That would be up to the runners. (Runners also would bring water as necessary, since we didn't have sinks.)

An assembly of about a hundred people was restricted to an area cordoned off near the room's entrance, identified as the "Guest Viewing Area" on the Bake-Off floor map. Our double row of marching cooks breezed past the crowd, the Doughboy and Sprout having positioned themselves as sentries at the gate.

The idea behind our processional, I think, was to take the longest possible route to find our ranges. I wound up and down an aisle or two before peeling off at my assigned location. There was no ambiguity about where I was supposed to be. In addition to #37, a placard was printed with "Ellie Mathews" and "Salsa Couscous Chicken." That could only be me.

My thirty-six-inch cabinet and workspace—like all others— had one drawer and one shelf behind a pair of doors. I opened the drawer. Rattling around, I found exactly the utensils I'd signed off on weeks before: a three-tined cooking fork, a nine-inch chef's knife, a set of measuring spoons, a measuring cup, a cutting board, and so forth. Seeing this little assortment of hardware made me feel at home. I knew what each piece was and what to do with it.

All around me ninety-nine other cooks made similar explorations into their cabinets, opening and closing drawers and doors, taking stock of various bits and pieces of kitchen hardware. Because this was it. The beginning of our moment.

Tentatively, I opened my cupboard doors. There was the frying pan I would need and a drawstring plastic bag with the Pillsbury logo printed on one side. Inside were all the ingredients I would need to make my chicken three times. Everything except the chicken. That was in the fridge. I lined everything up and checked it against my recipe, a copy of which, like everyone else's, had been taped to my countertop: a box of couscous, a small jar of honey, one garlic bulb, a bottle of cinnamon, one of cumin, a box of dried currants, a bag of almonds, a bottle of olive oil, two jars of Old El Paso Thick 'n Chunky Medium Salsa.

I wondered what would become of my unused ingredients. Clearly, nothing—not even salt—was coming from communal stores. I looked around at people opening fresh jars of mayonnaise, bottles of vinegar, cubes of butter. Everything was top quality. I watched a woman across the aisle withdraw a red pepper from her ingredients bag. It was the biggest, baddest red pepper I'd ever seen. She turned it over, inspecting each lobe, testing firmness with a practiced thumb.

The percussion of cabinet drawers and doors opening and

closing gave way to the furious sounds of chopping and frying. A not entirely pleasant bouquet of onion, chocolate, mushrooms, cinnamon, garlic, lemon, and sausage lifted into the air. Everyone around me seemed to be stirring, blending, slicing, frying, and generally going at it as if in a race.

We had until two o'clock. And I had my strategy from having watched the Olympics: Don't be first. Don't even be second.

The media had been held at bay while we familiarized ourselves with the setup, introduced ourselves to our runners and monitors, all of whom were easily identified in Pillsbury blue polo shirts and khaki pants. Now people in suits with clipboards were filtering in. Alex Trebek reappeared with a camera crew in tow. We had been told he would be conducting random interviews. I wanted him to interview me.

Another film crew was making its rounds for Pillsbury's requisite video moment with each of us. Since nothing was happening in my kitchen yet, I didn't attract attention from either crew. I looked at my watch. Nine twenty-five. My recipe necessarily took only thirty minutes, start to finish, for each batch. Those were the rules of the contest. Quick and Easy. If I made my dish three times, that would take me an hour and a half. Give me thirty minutes between each round to catch my culinary breath and some more minutes to fuss over doing an extra-special good job with the execution, and I'd still have slack time. Rather than chop my almonds with a rough hand, I could have carved them individually into representations of the U.S. presidents, or incised the Lord's Prayer on one or two for good measure. I had the knives to do it; Cutco supplied them sharp. One or two contestants had already explored the first-aid supplies.

I wandered out to the reception foyer and into the adjoining room, where breakfast had been replaced with a generous coffee and tea service. I felt both nervous and calm, cold and sweaty at once. No one else seemed to be delaying their start. Maybe my clammy skin was due to the hotel's aggressive HVAC, which made me feel chilled while I was, on the inside, slightly overheated. Always believing that hydration alleviates any ill, I helped myself to a bottle of water.

With the water in hand, I forced myself to review, one more time, the eight-by-ten-inch color glossies posted in the reception foyer. Brownies, appetizer bites, corn salads, soups, breads, pizzas, twists, tortes, tarts, cakes, cookies, and pasta blends of every stripe. My competition. The pictures had been up since our arrival, showing the results of Pillsbury's execution of all one hundred recipes, complete with food stylists' touches, such as the wink of a colorful napkin tucked under a plate or a cluster of vine-ripe tomatoes artfully placed off to the side.

My chicken would never be sexy looking. I hadn't called for parsley or cilantro or a slice of citrus to dress it up. Pillsbury's stylist and photographer had obviously done their best, having come in tight on a single thigh nestled into a bed of couscous at the edge of a turquoise-glazed terra-cotta plate. But the extreme close-up made the sauce look homely. The currants resembled something out of a medical illustration. The whole thing looked like police photography of an accident scene.

Opposite the photograph display was a long table with tiered risers and linen drapes, something like a rectangular wedding cake, where our dishes would accumulate throughout the day. Each of us had the choice of which of our dishes would be submitted for judging and which would be put up on this table for people to look at. The optional third batch would be for fellow cooks and members of the press to sample. If I burned one of my batches, I could dump it and still qualify. And, frankly, the outcome of the contest would not hinge on what the display batch tasted like—or looked like, since the judges would be sequestered far, far away from that draped table. So, really, out of my three tries, only one of them had to count. Still, pride dictated that I execute my recipe in earnest all three times.

I wasn't allowed to take my water bottle back in with me. I set it down half empty on a bus tray of dirty coffee cups and wandered back to my temporary home at No. 37 Bake-Off Lane.

To my immediate left was Helen Klecka, intent on her Apricot-Orange Chicken Picadillo. Like everyone's, a photocopy of her recipe as she'd submitted it was posted on her counter. Hers was a startling overlap with my own. We'd both qualified with a cup of Old El Paso Thick 'n Chunky Salsa. Where I'd used chicken thighs, she preferred breast meat. We both seasoned our dishes with cinnamon, although she used less of the spice than I. And while I sweetened with honey, she was using apricot preserves and frozen orange juice concentrate. She used almonds. So did I. She used raisins. I went for currants. The two of us cooking side by side offered living proof that there's not much new under the sun.

On my right, contest veteran Lisa Keys's Baja Shrimp Tacos smelled delicious. Like Helen and me, Lisa had qualified with Thick 'n Chunky Salsa. For a while I thought the room was organized by product. Then I decided we were segregated by cooking category—main dishes, appetizers, etc. Then I couldn't figure out any pattern.

Lisa, slender and pretty, seemed totally relaxed, maybe because she and her husband both work in the medical world as physicians' assistants. The Bake-Off probably seemed like a breeze compared to the life-and-death situations of her day-to-day existence. Besides, she and her husband had both participated in cook-offs before. I felt a little shy about talking to her, since she was obviously such a pro at competitive cooking. At the same time she seemed highly approachable.

"I quit entering contests with vacation packages for two as prizes," she told me. "We just don't want to go on all those trips without our kids. We're not comfortable pawning them off on relatives or babysitters for long periods of time."

Lisa turned back to her cooking. I was impressed she'd be in a position to pick and choose her contests. I was also impressed that she'd used mangoes in her tacos. So brilliantly fresh and tropical. Also, she was clearly a pro with the garnishing. Each of her wraps had a dollop of sour cream topped with mango, topped with cilantro. They looked good enough to eat.

The clock crept around to 10:30. I contemplated my range. The burners were electric. At home I cooked with gas, which I find more responsive. I had thought about this and devised a strategy.

A wood cookstove is the least responsive of all, and I was plenty experienced with those. In the early seventies, my sophisticated New York aunt, in a post-hippie, artsy, back-to-the-land sweep of life, installed herself in a primitive northern California homestead with no electricity, no phone, and only barely running water. When I visited her there I helped put the meals together, which, one year, included Thanksgiving dinner. In full Earth-Mother mode, I began that holiday by kneading bread dough, kindling a fire, and baking the loaf that would become the turkey's stuffing. Once the turkey was full of savory croutons, all I had to do was keep a steady glow in the firebox through the afternoon. With a woodstove, I learned that heat is controlled less by regulating the flame than by moving the pans around. High, low, and medium beneath a saucepan might be the front, back, and sides of the stove top. Oven temperatures are controlled with a complex of levered dampers and a few muttered incantations.

I knew before arriving in Orlando that the ranges would be electric. I had already decided to turn on all four burners to different degrees. That would give me the instant temperature regulation I was used to on my gas stove at home. All I'd have to do was move my pan around from one to the other as needed.

But Helen Klecka's bunch of parsley lay flopped onto my range. How could I heat up my two left burners under those curly green tops? I nudged them politely back into her territory. We had only six square feet each for workspace. It was a gargantuan bunch of parsley. She really didn't have the space for it by the time her ingredients were all spread out. I decided not to say anything because she might have been a little rattled by cooking in strange surroundings. I didn't want to derail her. I'd noticed a lot of very nervous cooks, and she might have been one of them. If so, she didn't need me pestering her. One woman I had talked to in the lobby told me that after she'd learned she was a finalist, she practiced making her pie *twenty-seven* times. The Bake-Off appeared to have her in such a ragged state, I just wanted to gather her up, hug her, and say: Let's hope no one gives themselves any heart attacks over this. I think it's *fun* that we get to be here at this wild party. Don't you?

I turned to my own operation. Time to take a run at the first round, even if only for my display requirement. I'd killed enough time. I knelt down to withdraw the big frying pan from my cupboard. By the time I stood up, however, there was the parsley again. Flopped onto my lower left burner.

Well, all I needed was a high and a medium. After the initial browning, I could reduce the hot one to a simmer and turn the other off. Let's not be fanatic about temperature control, I decided. I switched on my right front and right rear elements. I measured one tablespoon of high-class olive oil into my pan, ready to set on the heat. I peeled and minced two fat cloves of garlic. My first eight chicken thighs were about to hit the big time.

CHAPTER FOURTEEN

Months before, when recipes had poured into Pillsbury's mail room by the tens of thousands, the first level of judging was necessarily on paper. I guess if a recipe didn't read well, the assumption was that it wouldn't eat well. When I had typed mine to put in the mail, I imagined neatness would count, that a well-designed and carefully laid out page would make a difference. Wandering around the contest floor, however, gave evidence to the contrary. Some of the photocopies taped to finalists' counters had been submitted in difficult penmanship; others were poorly typed.

Mine, in a favorite—but neutral—typeface called Optima, had the recipe name at the top in all caps. Having worked as a graphic designer, I probably fussed more over the appearance of my entry than the recipe itself. I didn't like the name I'd dashed off, but I hadn't been able to think of anything witty. Salsa Couscous Chicken didn't exactly roll off the tongue, but at least each of the three words carried its own, descriptive weight.

Although this entry was a last-minute afterthought to the other submissions on which I'd spent more time and attention, I would not say its ingredients were selected at random—not because I had any edge on how to make it to the Bake-Off but because they are food items I generally I keep on hand and feel comfortable using.

Recognizing that cooks across America might not routinely stock couscous in their pantries, I tried some sleight-of-hand that I'd noticed while reading past winning recipes. At the head of my ingredients list I wrote, *3 cups hot, cooked couscous (rice may be substituted if couscous is not available).* By saying "cooked," I didn't have to repeat instructions for how to prepare a product that usually comes with instructions. And the suggested rice substitution was to get me off the hook with any judge who might have thought couscous was too exotic an ingredient.

Next came my nine other ingredients. Contest rules had it that everything should be listed in order of use.

Olive oil. If someone didn't get the message with the couscous that this recipe has Mediterranean roots, this was intended to help set the stage. Any old vegetable oil would have probably done the trick, but olive oil was thematic. Besides, that's what I keep next to my stove.

Chopped almonds. These could have just as easily been pine nuts, which might have been more authentic in the North African sense, but which seemed potentially more risky in terms of middle American acceptance. They are also not as widely available as almonds and they're pricier, too. I wanted to believe it would work in my favor if I kept a lid on the cost of ingredients.

Garlic cloves. I called for fresh.

Eight chicken thighs, skin removed. Because it has a higher fat content, chicken dark meat is more forgiving than breast meat. Since it's impossible to predict who's going to stick a microphone in your face at a critical moment while cooking under the spotlight, I thought it best to go with the most flexible ingredients possible, ones that are hard to ruin. In my experience, chicken breast meat has a twenty second window between being undercooked and turning into hard, dry, mealy clunks. Besides, thighs were what I had rattling around in the back of the freezer the day I first threw the recipe together. Why change what already works?

Old El Paso Homestyle Garden Pepper Salsa, mild or medium. I couldn't decide, so I left the option open. Piquancy is such an individual matter of taste. For the contest I flipped a virtual coin and asked for mild. In the Bake-Off cookbook, Pillsbury suggested Thick 'n Chunky as an alternate.

Dried currants. Zante currants and raisins are both little brown shriveled things. Except for the fact that a raisin is about ten times the size of a dried currant, one could think them interchangeable. To me they are not. When plumped and wet, I find raisins a bit on the squishy, baggy side. On the other hand, dried currants, when plumped, stay satisfyingly globular *sans* wrinkles. Technically, I should have distinguished the dried Corinth grapes that become Zante currants from actual currants, which are not grapes at all, but extremely tart berries—either red, white, or black—that are typically used fresh or made into jam or jelly. To add to the complication, the larger dried Thompson seedless grapes that we generally call raisins are called sultanas in other parts of the English-speaking world, but I wasn't using any of those.

Honey. I probably could have specified granulated sugar—or blackstrap molasses, for that matter—to achieve the same outcome, but, as with the olive oil, honey was thematic and intended to bolster the Moroccan theme. I called for a tablespoon, but this measure was an estimate, since I generally squirt out a glob and eyeball the amount rather than sticky up a spoon.

And, finally, the seasonings. Here, there could be no substitutes. *Cumin* and *cinnamon* in concert practically scream North Africa, and they are powerful enough to grab the Mexican-ness of the salsa by the throat and force it into submission. I can't take credit for any of this. The recipe for braised halibut with Middle Eastern spices that I had clipped from the *Seattle Times* years before provided my inspiration.

It might be easy to surmise, based on the components of my recipe and their analysis, that I knew precisely what I was doing when it came to entering the Bake-Off. But I didn't. My choices were the result of having put some sort of functional dinner on the table most nights over the three-plus decades that I'd been a mother and/or somebody's wife. Add to my on-the-job experience an inclination to be opinionated about food. Add to that my general impatience and a willingness to experiment and the results are invariably no-fuss but with a twist. I guess you could call me a something-from-nothing cook, always of the belief that the components of a meal are to be found somewhere between the pantry and the fridge. I rarely compile a shopping list; I never write out a week's menus. I go to the market, buy what looks good, and figure out how to put it all together once I'm home. So far, that system has worked out for me. Someday I may get caught having to make a four-course meal out of a can of clams, half a jar of Gerber's strained prunes, three dill pickles, and an artichoke.

In a 9 or 10 inch skillet, lightly sauté the almonds in the oil. Push almonds to one side. Add garlic. Stir and cook for 30 seconds or so. Add chicken thighs and brown over medium high heat for about 4–5 minutes, turning once.

Add salsa, cumin, cinnamon, honey, currants, and water. Stir well. Reduce heat to medium. Cover and cook for fifteen minutes or until juice runs clear from chicken when pierced with a fork.

Serve with couscous (or rice). Serves 4.

This is exactly how I cooked in Orlando. Step-by-step, I followed the recipe as I'd written it. I had to. Monitors were lurking around to make sure none of us pulled a fast one. Not that I would have changed a thing.

Actually, I would have changed one thing: my presentation. Not having called for a garnish was going to count against me big time. But I accepted my fate. My recipe had gotten me to Orlando and that had been my goal, pure and simple. I reminded myself I was at the Bake-Off on reconnaissance, gathering intelligence for next time when I'd do things right.

MY actual recipe preparation in that big, air-conditioned room with its swirl of media and chatter felt strangely anticlimactic. One might think this would be the time for me to feel the maximum drama, but it was not. I performed by rote. My ingredients couldn't be altered; my cooking methods had been cast in stone by virtue of the rules. All I had to do was read, measure, stir, wait, and serve. Meanwhile, Pillsbury had placed a straight-backed chair at each kitchenette, should any of us feel the need to give our feet a rest between the rigors of cooking.

I did not rest. I had already taken full advantage of wandering up and down the aisles to see what others were up to. I called on my new friend Penny and her snazzy asparagus salads at her range. I felt sorry for her immediate neighbor, a woman with a chocolate cake on the counter, one that appeared to have fallen, wet and sunken in the center. Maybe she had opened the oven door too many times during baking. Maybe she rushed things. Maybe she would salvage the situation on her second try.

Some cooks were cool as the cucumbers they were slicing; others appeared to be struggling. Rose Weikel, who had been carried off to the hospital from Planet Hollywood, was cooking her

Apple Crunch Coffee Cake from a wheelchair. I was glad to see her back among us, given the rumor that it had been her lifelong dream to be in the Bake-Off. Farther along I admired a couple of recipes-in-progress. Candice Merrill from Pasadena, California, had a clever idea: Pumpkin Bread Pudding with Ginger Cream, using Progresso bread crumbs as her qualifying ingredient. The results looked and smelled great, baggy raisins and all. Various people had cleverly dunked and rolled refrigerated biscuit dough in various combinations of melted butter, sugar, nuts, and cinnamon to stack and pack into coffee rings, cakes, and loaves. After having struggled to come up with my own ideas for what to do with prefab biscuits way back when, it was interesting to see others' inspirations.

Meanwhile, back at 37 Bake-Off Lane, my temporary home turf, Salsa Couscous Chicken was about to happen. My only strategy was to be absolutely methodical, checking and rechecking myself against my recipe as it was written. My bugaboo with presentation nagged at me, but there was nothing I could do about that. There were only three components on my platter and the couscous was going to match the glaze of the china, while the chicken and the sauce blended in with each other. Oh, for something green, a spatter of chopped cilantro, a foof of parsley—trite as parsley might be. A chiffonade of fresh mint or a slice of lime would have done wonders to perk things up. Forget whether the flavors would have enhanced the dish. I had entered a beauty contest of sorts and the swimsuit phase was coming up.

I had left Seattle still on the fence about how to organize my dish for serving, not that I had many choices. Chicken in the center, ringed with couscous? On the side? I ended up deciding I'd have to play it by ear once I saw the actual platters Pillsbury would provide. All contestants were required to use the company-issued neutral serving pieces, thereby avoiding any complications resulting from the use of our own crockery. One of us might have packed a grandmother's heirloom Wedgwood in her carry-on, while another might have brought a stark, matte black pottery square for her assembly. Too much like apples and oranges when it comes to assigning marks for presentation, so Pillsbury (I think wisely so) leveled the playing field. They had checked with each of us ahead of time about whether we preferred bowls, plates, or platters. Those were our choices. All of them either white or clear glass.

The platters were oval, their exact size having been selected from a list of dimensions during the paperwork exchange in the run-up to my departure for Orlando. I withdrew one from my cupboard and piled the couscous in the middle of it. I encircled the couscous with the eight chicken thighs, bone side down. Then I scraped the sauce out of the skillet and into a puddle in the middle of the couscous and that was that. Others around me were in the act of constructing multiple garnishes with architectural precision. Way back in December I had come to terms with the fact that I'd blown my chances in the presentation department. I looked longingly at the abundance of Helen Klecka's parsley.

To snip off a surreptitious bit for my own purposes would have made my efforts less homely, but it would have also earned me an instant disqualification. But, oh, those curly, green leaves!

I had known better (in theory) than to overlook this step; the rules stated right up front that points would be given for presentation. And I was surrounded by example. Other cooks were putting their all into sprigs and twists and curls and dollops that looked mighty appealing.

I alerted my runner that I was ready to submit my dish to the display table. After delivering same and signing off on step one, I headed out to the ongoing buffet lunch that had taken the place of our coffee and tea setup. There might have been a hundred salad items and sandwich makings to choose from. My appetite was at zero, but it seemed wise to make myself nibble on something.

At about 12:30 I was heavy into chopping almonds for my next round of chicken—the one that would conceivably get me into the $2,000 prize category if my stars were in alignment—when Pillsbury's video team found me for my requisite interview. Their camera was rolling. I offered my name, rank, serial number and answered a few boilerplate questions such as what's-your-dish-called and tell-us-your-inspiration. And then came the interviewer's classic probe, "So, Ellie, tell us what makes yours a winning dish."

A virtual red flag waved in my brain. Forgetting for the moment that being a finalist was a win of sorts, I said to her and her camera, "Well, it's not established yet that this *is* a winning recipe." I didn't want to go on record predicting that I was going to come out on top, when there was every reason to believe that statistics were against me.

Understandably, the interviewer lost interest at that point. She wanted clever or cute or entertaining, and I hadn't delivered. Her questions came to a halt. The camera's red light went dark. The interviewer and her assistants checked me off their list and moved on, leaving me with my little pile of chopped almonds.

The fact that I hadn't risen to the occasion by being fun and snappy and upbeat put me in a mild funk. I added the almonds to my pan and maybe stirred them more vigorously than necessary. I added the chopped garlic. This is always a critical step. Garlic doesn't overcook gracefully. It turns bitter. My oil was too hot.

I don't know whether I burned the garlic that day, because I never tasted the results. I wasn't sure about the rules, whether it was okay to take a taste. I'd heard that some contests fault you for not serving the absolute total recipe. Would a missing tea-spoonful make a difference? Also, there was the hygiene thing to consider with a tasting spoon and whether anyone might think I'd returned the spoon to the pan. Anyway, I soldiered on, step-by-step as before, and began arranging everything on my second platter, as before. I signaled my runner, as before. For what it was worth, this mess of chicken was ready for judging.

I had already visited the curtained off corner of the room where a photographer was set up to document each cook with her (or his) submission prior to the food being put on display.

The scene felt quasilegal, like a jockey's weigh-in before a race. This was it. Yes, I'm Ellie Mathews. And this is Salsa Couscous Chicken. And, yes, I'd be glad to sit here, holding up my platter. Sit up a little straighter? No problem. Smile? You bet. Of the eight or nine exposures the photographer made of me in front of the blue curtain at that pivotal moment, the one Pillsbury would select shows me grinning like Lewis Carroll's Cheshire cat. Chicken thighs are chasing each other around the rim of the plain white platter, looking like so many hedgehogs, nose-to-toes.

Now, as if making a sort of escrow deposit with a neutral— but trustworthy—party, I handed my second platter to a runner. She escorted me to the judges' door, where I signed off on my submission and left her to deliver my platter into the room where a panel of experts would sniff and poke at what I'd made.

CHAPTER FIFTEEN

The cooking frenzy of nine, ten, and eleven o'clock made a sharp decline at about noon. Now, as I faced my stove for the third and final time with less than an hour to go before the clock stopped on our event, the room practically echoed, like that scene in the 1959 film *Black Orpheus* where an ancient, lone janitor in the corridor of Rio's Missing Persons Department wades ankle-deep in gently blowing papers, swirling an ineffectual broom through the documents.

Stacks of dirty dishes. Crumpled paper towels. Surplus ingredients—some spilled, some slopped—all cluttered up what had earlier been in apple-pie order. The media had thinned. The video team had completed its one-minute interviews. Alex Trebek was nowhere to be seen, and the majority of cooks had vacated their sinkless kitchens. Runners and monitors drifted about in matching blue polo shirts and crisp-pressed khakis.

I heated my burners one last time—not because it was required but because the ingredients were supplied and I thought they'd go to waste if I didn't use them. Also nagging at me was the desire to have someone realize that—humble as my dish may have looked—I had nothing to apologize for when it came to taste.

Pillsbury had stocked my cabinet with a quantity of small paper plates, plastic forks, and cocktail-size napkins. During the earlier hubbub, people had been grazing and nibbling back and forth up and down the aisles, trying each others' recipes. I hoped someone would want to try what I was making.

Salsa Couscous Chicken necessarily takes only half an hour to make, start to finish, including preparation and cooking. That was the maximum time allowed in my category, 30-Minute Main Dishes. All four categories were geared toward Quick and Easy, the theme of the contest.

By the time my last gasp of chicken was out of the pan and distributed among my dozen or so little paper plates, more people had vacated the Oceans Ballroom of the Renaissance Orlando Resort. It was looking, frankly, bombed out. Chairs were askew. A few drawers and cupboard doors had been left open.

A man with a loosened necktie approached. He looked tired. And maybe a little burned out on tasting everyone's best recipe.

"Would you care for a sample?" I said, offering him a plate. His badge identified him as a food editor with a Florida newspaper.

He took a tentative bite and made a sound. I couldn't tell whether it was "Hmmm?" or "Mmmm." There's a world of difference.

"Care to give me a critique?" I ventured. I'm a bit in awe of real, live food experts and I thought his might be the only professional evaluation I'd get out of the Bake-Off, once my entry had been passed over by the judges.

"It's good," he said. "Good." He seemed like a man who had sampled a lot of food in his career.

"Thank you. But how would you improve it?"

"Just one thing is all. It needs something green with it." He circled one hand over the remaining sample servings. "Chopped mint. Parsley or something." And with that he tipped his empty plate into the nearby trash can and was gone.

I was in seventh heaven. A *bona fide* foodie had found nothing to criticize except to confirm what I already knew. Hallelujah. I could go back to Seattle happy.

I looked about, eager to serve another sample or two or three. While I'd been chopping and stirring, I wondered whether I'd have enough to go around. With the exception of that lone food editor, however, the crowds weren't exactly lined up and waiting. Anything conceivably called a crowd was long gone. Three or four people at the far end of the room stood in a clump of conversation. I couldn't see chasing them down and interrupting for the sake of showing off. I fiddled around. I rolled down the inner wax wrap of my remaining currants; I tucked the cardboard tab of its box top closed. I screwed tight the lids on my jars of salsa and honey; I stacked my sticky measuring spoons and my cutting board and other equipment into my dirty frying pan to make it easier for someone to take them to be washed. I folded my dish towel and squared it up with the edge of the counter. I tucked the extra cocktail napkins into my apron pocket to take home. They had Pillsbury's blue logo printed on them and seemed worth keeping as souvenirs.

Meanwhile, my hopeful little servings of chicken and couscous congealed. In the end I unceremoniously dumped them in the trash.

So much for making use of the ingredients.

Okay. The cooking was over and it felt just a teeny bit anticlimactic. I don't know that I was the absolute last person to finish up, but I was somewhere close to last. My departure from that hundred-stove room and its miles of electrical cables differed markedly from my entrance earlier that morning. There was no throbbing disco music. No Pillsbury Doughboy offering high fives. George and Sally had repaired to parts unknown. Nobody with a clipboard said good-bye to me. No one checked me out or off. No one was posted to make sure I wasn't hijacking my leftover almonds.

I loitered in the foyer ready to make small talk with the few people orbiting the display table. I didn't want to appear too eager to be part of the group, but if there was anything approaching a group at all, I wanted to become part of it.

At the long, draped table, each dish was accompanied by a card with the recipe name and the name of its creator. Mine was mercifully all the way at the end, next to the wall. I went around to the other side. There, in slot 66, was the sunken-in chocolate cake I'd seen earlier. One slice was pulled out for display. A top-knot of cream supported one perfect mint leaf.

"Oh, *this* poor woman," I said to no one in particular.

"Yeah, she's predicted to win," a man near me said.

I reevaluated the cake's moist center. "Oh," I said, "it's *meant* to be like that." The card read, "Brownie Soufflé Cake with Mint Cream."

"She's a pro," someone said.

"Oh," I said.

"Edwina Gadsby. Her husband's here, too."

"Oh," I said. "As a finalist?"

"He made Crab Cakes Italiano. Together those two have won, like, hundreds of contests."

"Oh."

So much for my evaluation of a fallen cake.

We were heading into the shank of the afternoon, with time to kill before our next scheduled event. By now, I was confident that it would be another extravaganza. Just because we'd completed the nitty-gritty of this cooking event, Pillsbury wasn't about to leave us twiddling our thumbs on the last night. Another party was planned, this one at Universal Studios. Silly me, before the Bake-Off I had thought Universal Studios was a movie company in California and not a theme park in Florida.

My health had improved, but I was feeling at loose ends. I thought a swift walk might help me re-align my molecules and set my internal psychic gauges back to neutral. I've always believed in the benefits of a brisk walk, even when it takes place along a whizzing interstate or whatever that traffic corridor was behind the hotel. Never mind the lack of a destination, walking for walking's sake usually straightens out my kinks when they need straightening. I'd been on my feet all day, of course, but that's not the same as a little heart-thumping exercise.

Upstairs in my room I stashed my apron and freshened up. My window was level with palm fronds slapping against each other in an ominous thrum. That and the coarse-textured lawn of the south were botanical reminders that I was in the land of exotic species. I remembered reading about a boy in the sixties who smuggled three giant African land snails from Hawaii into Miami. His grandmother subsequently released this kid's pets into her garden. A few years later, their progeny were sliming up the countryside by the thousands. Not wanting to bump into any of these fist-sized mollusks, I cleaned my glasses.

I went out the side door of the hotel, sort of a porte cochere arrangement off the sublobby taken up with Bake-Off activities. Out in the open, the banging of the palm fronds was louder. Some serious wind had kicked up. They weren't coconut palms, but I had an image of getting conked on the head by falling objects. Suddenly, walking didn't seem like such a good idea after all.

CHAPTER SIXTEEN

It felt completely normal for me to vacillate between hoping I'd win a prize at the Bake-Off and fearing I might. Sometimes I lurch into things while simultaneously hesitating. I accelerate while applying the brakes to a situation, not sure I meant to move forward to begin with. In Orlando I had dared to aim one foot toward the spotlight while keeping the other planted firmly in shadow. Now, the afternoon of the third day, cooks had cooked, and—as far as we knew—judges had judged. The deed was done. We would wait overnight to learn the outcome, at which point Alex Trebek would reappear to administer the televised awards show. Nothing anyone could do now would alter the results. Chocolate had been meticulously drizzled, onions had been diced to geometric precision and carefully frizzled. Noodles had been boiled, cream had been whipped; cheddar had been grated, spinach had been steamed, pies had been sliced; cakes had been glazed; and various biscuit sticks had been twisted, baked, and cinnamon-sugar dipped.

The wind was whipping up to a higher pitch. Upstairs, outside my room, palm fronds spanked and stung the air with increasing vigor. Someone on the television news used the word *tornado*. I didn't know what to make of that. Where I live in the Northwest, tornadoes are virtually unheard of. Our natural disasters are more likely to be earthquakes and volcanoes. But a twister? I looked briefly under the desk Marriott had furnished the place with and imagined crouching beneath it, but instead I decided to carry on as scheduled while hoping for the best.

Buses showed up to take us to Universal Studios for our third and final blowout. Unlike our earlier trips to Disney World and Planet Hollywood, this party included the entire Bake-Off population, not just the finalists and their guests but the runners, the monitors, the behind-the-scenes personnel, people from Whirlpool, Cutco, and KitchenAid, people who had strung the miles of electrical wires to power our stoves, had shopped for—and stocked our cupboards with—our jars of mayonnaise, cans of tomatoes, bulbs of garlic, boxes of powdered sugar. These men and women were at the Bake-Off to work. They had muscled our temporary kitchens into place, had acted as floor assistants, contest explainers, hosts and organizers, Band-Aid appliers. They had generally kept things going smoothly, and this evening would be part of their reward for jobs well done. It was their party, too.

A couple hundred of us milled around at Marriott's porte cochere, waiting to board the buses. Through the gathering dusk I saw Penny Nichols's familiar face across the way, but she appeared to have coupled up with someone else for the ride. I contented myself again with the thought that I'd given the Bake-Off my body but not my soul; I was still prepared to go it alone.

That's when Amy Giovanini entered the picture. If I believed in providential intervention or guardian angels, I'd say she was one. I could almost believe that someone in the Pillsbury organization had slipped her a Price-Waterhouse sealed envelope and assigned her the task of plucking me from the crowd with the specific intention of drawing me out of my shell and warming me up for what was to come. Except, as I would learn later, the Pillsbury judges were still tearing their hair out at that point anyway.

Amy offered me the empty seat beside her. She introduced herself as a group marketing manager in Pillsbury's refrigerated dough division. Until the Bake-Off I'd never even heard of canned pizza crust, although I did have a vague recollection of experimenting with a cardboard tube of Danish pastries when I was first married.

As the bus pulled away from the curb, we slid into easy conversation. Like the Progresso marketing manager I had sat beside at our banquet the first night, I discovered that Amy also liked to go exploring in new grocery stores.

"Me, too," I said. "It's practically a spectator sport. You never know what you might find. Like in the South once, I saw a big heap of fresh black-eyed peas. Fresh. Still in the pod. Who would think? I'd only ever seen them dried. Or canned. But I guess they have to grow somewhere."

Amy was pretty and young and vivacious and had that beguiling appearance of being absolutely comfortable in her own skin. I was probably older than her mother. But, buoyed by Amy's élan and easy familiarity, I felt immediately in the swing, propelled by the beat of the brass band that greeted us as we got off the bus.

"Let's try everything," she said as we neared the entry gate.

"I'm not sure what everything would involve," I said. We flashed our special Bake-Off VIP badges to the admissions guard.

"Who cares? It'll be fun." Amy took me by the hand and actually pulled me along.

Pillsbury had bought out the theme park for the evening. We began with a reception at the Beetlejuice Courtyard. I saw Penny across the crowd again and waved to her. Amy called out and waved to her friends. She talked to anyone and everyone within a six-foot radius, weaving me into her instant societies. She nudged me forward.

This was not a night for pinky fingers and frilly teacups. Festivities were off and running with beer and every kind of chip. Gargantuan mountains of calorific indulgence all beckoned on huge tables encircling the courtyard. There were endless heaps of chips—with and without ridges, with and without barbecue, onion, cheddar powder. There were Fritos, pretzels, tortilla crisps—with and without seasoning—fries, twists, crunchies. It was junk food mania. Although I avoid fat when cooking, my gastronomic Achilles' heels when snacking happen to be salt and grease. I dove for the pile of pumpkin-colored cheese curls, practically Day-Glo with their FD&C Yellow No. 6 turning my fingers wonderfully and monstrously orange.

Someone said Pillsbury's parent company owned Harp and Guinness. That was a good enough reason to sample them both, a pair of old reliables as far as I'm concerned, a couple of good friends. I'm nuts about good beer.

Our crowd spilled into the theme park's diminutive street. I felt the excitement of our group, one that had been holding its collective breath for a long, long while. Tonight, it was time to exhale. Word rustled among us that a Mardi Gras parade would be coming through. People began positioning themselves along the curb and cocking their heads toward the thread of New Orleans jazz wafting down the avenue. Amy edged me toward the front row.

"I can see okay from here," I said.

"Don't you want to catch whatever they'll be throwing?"

Someone in an outlandish costume, high up on a parade float, tossed candy coins and strings of beads into our crowd's eager hands. They were the sort of sweets and trinkets that eventually get thrown away, but there I stood at the front, arms straining to snag the momentary thrill of shiny objects.

Then we were off to explore Universal Studios' carnival of activities, including free access to the movie-themed rides the place is famous for—complete with warnings posted for anyone who might be faint of heart. After that, we were treated to a New

York–style street party with the Blues Brothers Dance Band and a spectacular buffet set up like market vendors' carts offering every class of food and drink and sweet.

If only it hadn't been so windy, I might have stayed longer. But tablecloths flapped ominously, and our hair blew across our mouths and eyes.

By the time the bus returned us to the Renaissance Resort, I was barely thinking of what might happen the next day in terms of Bake-Off prizes. The television news was full of tornado predictions. Still high on the evening's excitement, I took a hefty swig of cough syrup, crawled into bed, and wondered how much structural steel had been incorporated in the hotel's walls.

Tomorrow I'd be going home.

Chapter Seventeen

The awards show was to be televised. Pillsbury had bought thirty minutes of air time from CBS to run live from 11:00 until 11:30 EST Tuesday morning, after which contestants would begin shuttling to the airport. In our advance instructions, finalists had been asked to "wear something nice" the last day. All of us would be on camera briefly and a few would be in the spotlight.

I dusted off my television clothes and flicked on the morning news. Tornados had touched down after all. A reporter stood in the rubble of a trailer park that had been upended. Those red lines I'd seen on the weather chart the night before had become reality, no longer mere map symbols of where the tornados were predicted to hit but actual streaks across the land. I instinctively went to the window. Winter Park, the reporter continued, had been one of the communities torn apart. Less than ten miles from where I stood, Winter Park was the community where Carl and I had always stayed when we worked for the Florida-based computer company, but I had never been anywhere near a tornado during those visits. A video clip showed where tractor trailers had been blown off the highway. In all, forty-two people had died, and hundreds more were injured. One of the fatalities, an elderly priest asleep in his chair, had been hurled from one side of the street to the other.

From my window I could see nothing out of order. Palm trees stood upright. People at ground level were going about their routines. The new day appeared as full of promise as any. The frivolity of my immediate concerns about how to dress for a live broadcast stood in sharp contrast to those in the path of nature's forces. Two ways to be featured on television.

Including the lucky shirt, my Bake-Off wardrobe was a combination of Goodwill bargains and clothes from Opus 204, a hopelessly expensive Seattle boutique. I usually feel confident in their clothes. In some settings the simple lines and smart fabrics their designer chooses actually make me feel elegant, like the silk PJs I wore for the banquet or the oversized canvas jacket I'd worn to Universal Studios to shield myself from the wind. The generous cut of thick cotton I'd chosen for the awards day, however, just looked baggy and out of place when I saw it reflected in the hotel mirror. The designer at Opus had called it French terry cloth, which sounded snazzy at the time, but the tunic and leggings suddenly made me feel lumpy. They seemed irrevocably beige. Good thing I had no illusions about being singled out for any camera close-ups. At least I was neat and clean, no loose threads or safety-pinned hems. I'd be leaving for home immediately after the show, and, if the truth be known, I was more fixed on being in comfortable clothes for my long flight to Seattle than on how I might look on Toshiba screens across the nation.

Breakfast was set up as before (and by that I mean lavishly) on the main floor, in a large room near where we had cooked. Afterward there was packing to see to. I filled out the oversized red, white, and blue Pillsbury tag and attached it to my suitcase to be put in the lobby for transporting to the airport. I decided to leave my handbag and jacket in my room until after the show. I'd have just enough time to comply with the hotel's 12:00 checkout time before leaving for my plane home. That way I wouldn't have to carry anything with me to the show, which was set up in the hotel's Crystal Ballroom on the main floor.

Seating for the one hundred contestants was assigned by range number. That would have me next to Lisa Keys again. Contestant guests would sit separately, along with the press, the judges, and the contest support staff. We were asked to be in place by 10:30 for the 11:00 broadcast. There was no margin for error. This was going to be live. Whatever happened in that time slot in that ballroom would happen across the airwaves.

The corral of suitcases in the hotel lobby at 10:00 was evidence that the party was almost over. We knew from our orientation instructions that the winner's luggage was to be pulled from the stack and routed to Los Angeles. Pillsbury already had a plane ticket for Person X to fly with Marlene Johnson and a PR specialist.

A few clutches of people stood anxiously around the arrangement of suitcases, hoping to see that their bags were missing—advance evidence of being the winner—but all bags seemed to be present. (I would learn later that Pillsbury was one jump ahead of this scheme. The critical suitcase wasn't going to be pulled until after we were seated and the broadcast had begun.)

The Crystal Ballroom was the hotel's showpiece, with ornate, mammoth chandeliers and mirrors on every wall. Hundreds of chairs arced in front of a stage set up like a cheery kitchen, complete with flowered wallpaper, cookbooks on the shelf, wine bottles, papier-mâché croissants, a faux window above a faux sink, and a Pillsbury Doughboy cookie jar on the counter. The living, breathing, eight-foot edition of the Doughboy rocked from foot to foot to the left of the stage. His green companion, Little Sprout, stood to the right, waving his three-fingered hands.

Every inch of floor space was jammed with TV equipment and technicians. Members of the press, and the contest's myriad support people, milled around. Obediently, I found my seat at 10:30 sharp. Being organized in rows by range number had us segregated by cooking category. We knew from our orientation meeting that under no circumstance were we to switch or sit out of place. I guessed this was so the camera operators—who must have known ahead of time who the winners were—could pick people out by location.

It was the last event of the Bake-Off. We'd been coached on

what was expected of those who would be named as winners. I settled in, happy to watch the proceedings and do what I'd been told. Or so I thought.

Like everything else Pillsbury had planned, our event was well choreographed. Nothing was left to chance. A professional warm-up man came on the scene to froth us up.

As soon as he had all eyes focused forward and moving in unison to his high-energy pitch, he orchestrated us to hold up our hands and rub our fingertips against our thumbs—something you wouldn't think would make a sound. There must have been three hundred or more people in the room. Turns out that's enough fingers that, when rubbed in unison, sound like a rainstorm. He directed us to sweep the sound from left to right then back again. I wanted to do it one more time.

But Mr. Warm-Up got down to more serious business. He told us Alex Trebek would appear in a few minutes to begin hosting the show. In keeping with the *Jeopardy!* format, we were to respond with a rehearsed answer when prompted with a question. Specifically, we were coached to yell *One. Mill-yun. Doll-urz!* on cue.

That brought out the rebel in me. I don't like to be told what to say or when to say it, pure and simple. Besides, fawning over money strikes me as undignified.

The crowd around me complied with direction when prompted: *"One. Mill-yun. Doll-urz!"* I felt confident that no one was going to notice or kick me out for sitting mute. I was there as an observer anyway. Wasn't that my main purpose—to see how the whole Bake-Off thing really played out?

Just short of 11:00, the lighting in the room changed, darker over the audience and brighter at the front. Alex Trebek bounded up, and the show was under way. Before saying anything to the camera about the Bake-Off, however, he unfolded the front page of that morning's *Orlando Sentinel*. The headline read, "Deadly Night," in the largest possible type, below which were color photographs of the same sort of tornado upheaval I'd seen on television.

"Pillsbury is not unmindful of the devastation," he said. "I'm sure I speak for all of you when I say our hearts go out to those who have suffered losses." Then he wished central Floridians a speedy recovery and said, "To help them, Pillsbury has donated five thousand cases of food." This elicited spontaneous and thunderous applause, which was a great segue to the particulars of the awards show.

Video monitors on either side of the stage showed a lively string of clips taken of us marching into the Bake-Off behind George and Sally, contestants checking over ingredients, contestants volunteering sound bites to Trebek's interview questions from the day before. I was dazzled at how much video production had taken place overnight. Those guys must have been sweating it out in the editing room while the rest of us had been guzzling beer at the Beetlejuice Courtyard and scaring ourselves silly at the King Kong-o-rama.

It was almost 11:15 before the first award was announced. There were no commercial breaks. The whole show was a commercial, when you came right down to it. Trebek outlined rules of the contest. Four semifinalists from each of the four categories would be named. During our Sunday orientation, we'd been asked to stand in place if our names were called at that point and to stay on our feet until directed to sit back down. My group, the 30-Minute Main Dish category, sat leftmost. Alex began with us.

He first named Westy Gabany from Olney, Maryland, for her Chicken Salad Focaccia Sandwiches. She leapt up, effervescent. Next, and coincidentally seated beside Westy, was Debbie Powyszynski from Allen, Texas, for her Speedy Spinach Squares Alfredo. Westy and Debbie grabbed each other, squealed, and jumped up and down.

Then I heard my own name. I couldn't believe it. Wow! All of this and $2,000 to take home on top of it. I had barely dared to hope for this. I was too far from anyone I knew to exchange hugs and squeezes. Lisa Keys gave me a congratulatory pat, but I didn't feel connected enough with her to involve her further in my delight—it would have felt presumptuous—so I just stood there and endured a burst of applause.

Finally, Ellen Nishimura, from Fair Oaks, California, stood for her Seven-Layer Chinese Chicken Salad.

Westy, Debbie, Ellie, Ellen. One of us would be called as a finalist and would win not just two thousand dollars but ten. That was a given.

We were directed to sit back down, and Alex introduced the next category.

This same drama of naming four semifinalists from each cooking category was played out three more times until four groups of four had had a turn in the limelight, the category announcements interspersed with video insets of what the entries looked like in their finished state.

The clock was ticking on our half-hour show. Not until the broadcast was more than two-thirds of the way along was it time to advance to the next level.

"Now the action really heats up," said Trebek, figuratively biting a fingernail or two. He was expert at building the tension. "We are just minutes away from awarding our one-million-dollar cash prize." He paused before adding, "Will our sixteen semifinalists please stand up again, because we're ready to announce the winning recipe in each category."

Rising one more time I tried to be a good sport about following instructions. Spotlights swam from one to the other of us, swirling. This few seconds on my feet would be my last official Bake-Off performance, after which I would fade back into being part of the audience. I was already thinking forward to the trip home and how I'd regale Carl with all the details and how—guess what?—I'd won us two thousand dollars.

CHAPTER EIGHTEEN

Trebek's delivery, at first, had sounded entirely spontaneous. Then I glanced to the main camera and saw someone flipping poster board cue cards like so many slices of cheese. I considered feeling cheated by the artifice of television. But Trebek was smooth and convincing; I lost interest in tracking where his lines were coming from. I simply let the proceedings carry me along.

Now, sixteen of us had been singled out, and we were on our feet. This was no artifice.

As with the semifinalists, the 30-Minute Main Dish finalist would be named first. I listened to hear which of the others would be called. But there was *my* name, hanging like glitter in the air: "Will Ellie Mathews! from Seattle, Washington! join me onstage!"

My seat was somewhat "inland" from the aisle. I struggled

my way across ten pairs of feet in the second row, trying not to mash anyone's toes as I went. A woman at the end of the aisle touched my arm in a reassuring way. I lurched toward the stage, my limbs not entirely under graceful control. I climbed three or four stairs to Trebek's level. As the first finalist up there I had no one to hide behind or mimic in terms of how or where to stand. I hoped to heaven I was positioned where Pillsbury wanted me to be. Details at this level had not been covered in the orientation. I felt like someone who had been watching a black-and-white movie when the cinematographer switched to wide-screen color film.

Someone handed Trebek an envelope. "From the Simple Side Dishes category," he boomed out from the card within, "our finalist is Betty Schroedl! from Jefferson, Wisconsin! for her Texas Two-Step Slaw!"

Betty had made a cole slaw that I thought sounded terrific, with Green Giant corn, cilantro, lime, cumin, and cheddar added to the cabbage. She had also given it a clever name. I winced again at the utilitarian name I had chosen for my chicken.

Betty might have been in her seventies, she moved quickly enough, but it seemed an eternity for her to make her way to the stage and take a place at my side. I squeezed her hand upon arrival; I wanted acknowledgment that we were both in this together, but she did not squeeze back.

"In the Fast and Easy Treats"—Trebek had opened another envelope—"congratulations to Edwina Gadsby! of Great Falls, Montana! the creator of the Brownie Soufflé Cake with Mint Cream!"

So the predictions were coming true. That was the first time I'd connected the cake with the face of its inventor. Edwina was a meringue of dimples and blond curls in a colorful scarf. Unlike me, she *had* worn television clothes. Apparently she really was the pro that everybody said she was. Edwina exchanged smiles with me as she arrived to cling to the edge of television's kitchen along with Betty and me.

"And our finalist in the Quick and Easy Snacks and Appetizer category is Richard McHargue! of Richmond, Kentucky! for his Tex-Mex Appetizer Tart!"

McHargue, one of the two men I had shushed during our orientation meeting, wore a short-sleeved dress shirt, open at the collar. He raised both fists into the air in a gesture of triumph before bounding to the stage. He was long-boned enough that it seemed to take him only a couple of strides to reach us, and he burst into an excited hug with Edwina before falling into the last place in our tight little lineup. His tart involved a prepared pie crust, mayonnaise, melted cheese, and canned chilies.

One, two, three, four. We stood on display. But wait. The Whirlpool Quick and Easy prize diverted attention. Carmen Hunter of Clearwater, Florida, had added flaked coconut, vanilla, and coconut extract to a tube of refrigerated cookie dough to make White Chocolate Macaroons. Her recipe was judged the easiest to prepare and was awarded the only noncash prize, a collection of new kitchen appliances valued at $5,000. While Carmen stood beaming at her place in the audience, the heat was temporarily off our foursome onstage.

That gave me a chance to gather my wits, such as they were. I found it harder and harder to stick with my statistical approach to things. Three of us would not end up in first place, but it seemed more likely than 75 percent that I would be one of those three. I believed I simply hadn't made that clever a dish. On the other hand, being present on that stage meant I'd be taking home ten grand.

The clapping for Carmen subsided.

Marlene Johnson had described at our orientation meeting how the winning recipe would be revealed. Rather than announcing the name, someone would bear a domed platter to the stage. Under the dome would be the million-dollar dish.

Only one more announcement remained. Alex turned to Betty, Edwina, Richard, and me. "Nervous?" he asked with a knowing grin. Richard and Edwina, who stood closest to him, both nodded with trepidation like a pair of people about to bungee jump from a bridge. Meanwhile, the woman in the neat teal-green suit, who had touched my arm as I made my way to the stage, was bearing Pillsbury's domed platter up the same stairs that I had climbed. She set down the gigantic platter with its gleaming silver dome, set it on the counter on which the four of us were stabilizing ourselves. The winning dish was concealed right under our noses.

Strangely enough, I wasn't nervous—unless you count the garden-variety anxiety of being onstage (and national television). I still felt as if I were watching someone else's event. I knew I didn't belong up there. I felt something of a fraud—a gate-crasher—but

I was delighted to have such a close-up view of the goings-on. I couldn't imagine winning; I'd made mistakes, hadn't practiced over and over at home as others had. Plus, there was the garnish factor: my lack of parsley.

On the other hand, that platter borne by the woman in green looked heavier than it might have if all it held was a small cake on a small plate. Heavy enough for four American-sized servings of chicken with all its salsa couscous fixings. You can tell sometimes. It looked heavy.

The audience settled down to a rumble of anxious expectation. A quick video review of each of our finished dishes increased tension with its diversion. The show was almost over, and the air felt more charged than ever. I prepared myself to congratulate one of the other three—probably Edwina, maybe Betty—after which I would return to my seat.

And then a drumroll. Trebek grabbed the looped handle of the giant dome but did not lift. He let a pregnant pause elapse. And then, with flair, he raised up that oval cover in a flash.

"Salsa Couscous Chicken!"

I almost didn't know what I was looking at, arranged as I'd arranged it yesterday. How did anyone know? How did *my chicken thighs* get in there? Where was the chocolate cake? I half expected the Pillsbury people to rush in and set things straight, replace the chicken with the brownie soufflé, make apologies for the dreadful mix-up. A big corporate goof. But no such rush occurred. Just applause.

I'd won.

But how? My brain couldn't keep pace with my heart. Time became elastic, moving too fast while also in slow motion. I felt both semiconscious and hyperconscious at once. I clung to funny details like the scent of soap on Alex Trebek's hands, and the glimpse of Amy Giovanini's face in the acres of faces in front of me. The sight of her was a welcome flash of something familiar, almost like an anchor in a current too strong to swim against.

I should have thought forward to the possibility of this moment. I'd wanted to win only in the most abstract sense, competition for competition's sake; I hadn't considered the consequence of being onstage, or being featured on television. I wasn't prepared.

I hung on to the security of that white kitchen counter as long as I could. I shook my head in denial, wishing I could fade into the cheery wallpaper of the set. The audience rose to their feet in ovation. Alex, in the nicest possible way, pulled me to the front of the stage. He said, "Come on out here. You've won a million dollars!" I couldn't get myself to show any of what I was feeling. I'm not sure I even *knew* what I was feeling. Only that something cosmic had just occurred, and that the something didn't come supplied with a script. Alex whispered that it might be a good idea for me to hug him. Why hadn't I thought of that myself? Of course. His coaching eclipsed my inclination to hold out both hands, palms to the audience like brakes to say, *Just kidding, everyone. I only came here to catch the first act.* So I hugged Alex instead.

Accepting me as if I were a rag doll, Trebek initiated a big squeeze. His maroon blazer felt uncommonly soft against my cheek. Cashmere? I wondered. I supposed with his success he could buy any kind of fine clothes he wanted. Why was I so focused on his jacket of all things? Like a victim of a car crash recalling the incident after the fact, the details that stood out now seem totally random.

I have wished that I could play those moments over—not for the glory of the win, but to be more present to the experience. If any of us could predict, however, when lightning was going to strike, the world would be an entirely different place.

CHAPTER NINETEEN

Although I was sharply aware that the prize money didn't actually come from Alex Trebek at all—that he was neither judge nor sponsor—I thanked him. I thanked him again and perhaps again. One of those times I was thanking him with all my heart for guiding me through the intensity of the drama.

A few seconds remained of the broadcast. Credits rolled and the background music rose. Through the continuing applause, Alex said to me—audible through the fade of our microphone, "You're going to be able to devote a lot of time to that writing fellowship now."

He must have taken a look at my background questionnaire where I'd listed a few of my achievements, although that fellowship had been a one-time honor, now long in the past. The audience remained standing with its ovation. In response to the cheering, I hugged Trebek again, this time spontaneously. Then I took refuge behind the safe haven of the set's island kitchen to shake hands with the other three finalists, beginning with Edwina. Trebek, too, shook hands all around before turning back to me and asking, "Did your husband come with you?"

Remembering how Carl and I had discussed my making the trip solo, I offered a clumsy explanation, "No. We looked on this as sort of a business trip." Clumsy wasn't the word for it; my response didn't come out at all the way I'd meant it. I intended it to be an apology for not doing things right, for not being in the swing of things, for being a party-pooper, a penny-pincher, for not knowing how to play along. Why I thought he would understand my terminology is a mystery. From his perspective I had exhibited almost no emotion at the point of impact, and then I turned around and equated the experience to a *business* trip.

Thinking back on it, I wish I'd simply explained that Carl had been to Florida before or that I saw myself as a Bake-Off outsider and not ready to jump in with both feet. I wish I'd explained that I never fantasized such a dramatic outcome and therefore hadn't anticipated the need for my husband's stabilizing presence.

Trebek took one giant step back. The combination of my freeze-up at the winning moment with the notion of a business trip could have given the impression of ultra-calm. Or even calculating. Hard boiled, maybe. I hadn't shrieked or whooped or gasped or let out so much as a peep at the moment of impact. He didn't know I was too stunned.

When I think of that moment I cringe. No one wants to see an ungracious winner. Of all my bumbling and subsequent mumblings in the interviews that followed, I regret giving such a wrong impression in that one instance. Maybe the immediate sting of not having made myself clear gave rise to my super caution in the press conference that followed.

Before the press interviews, however, there were checks to hand out. The television cameras had powered down, but the audience was asked to remain. Paul Walsh, CEO of Pillsbury, came forward. He was the money man. All the winners were called to the stage to be named and congratulated one more time, each receiving an envelope from Walsh, all of the winners basking in continuing applause. All of *us*, if you include me.

I felt dazed. It was time for most of the audience to vacate—they had planes to catch—but the reporters stayed. They crowded and buzzed. Finally, I was released from the stage. A man in a suit broke out of the crowd, approached me, and asked advice on what I believed was most critical to winning a contest. It seemed incumbent on me to say something intelligent. Me, now a spokesperson for all things competitive. I struggled to try to gather a clear thought but managed only a few croaks. Then the man broke into a grin and said, "Entering. You can't win unless you enter," and he and his suit faded back into the crowd. It was a trick question, intended as a joke, and I just stood there like a dope.

Someone produced champagne and real glasses and strawberries to float, a nice gesture, but I knew better than to accept.

It wasn't even nine in the morning on my bio-clock, which still ticked to Pacific Standard Time. I needed all the wits I could assemble to make my way through the unexplored territory of the day ahead.

Additionally, there was the medicine I was taking for my pneumonia. My pills were probably compatible with alcohol, but I wasn't sure. As for the cough syrup I'd been chugging, that one did say to use care when operating dangerous machinery. Good advice in any situation.

A press conference can be equated to dangerous machinery. At the front of the stage, a chair appeared, and I was ushered back up the stairs to sit. An ocean of reporters assembled before me. I floated. I don't know whether it was ego or practicality or fear, but I realized with perfect clarity that anything I might say could show up in print, and I was acutely aware that spontaneous responses don't always play well on the page. Cameras flashed. Somewhere in the back of my mind, a voice reminded me to choose my words carefully. I Mirandized myself: anything you say can and will be used against you. I remember saying that winning a million dollars felt weird in a good way and that it would take a while for it all to sink in. Some reporters laughed. Others looked blank. Still others repeated the question as if I'd somehow supplied the wrong answer.

Later I would learn it's possible to reply to a reporter's question by answering the question you wish you'd been asked, and they won't call you on morphing the topic. For now, however, I was doing my best to reply with all the earnestness and candor I could muster.

"So how does it feel to be an instant millionaire?" came a woman's voice from the back.

"Terrific," I said. "But very abstract."

"No, but how does it *feel*?" she asked again, and it occurs to me now how natural it was for her to try for a better answer. *Abstract* isn't really a feeling, is it? She wanted a peek at my emotional state, and I'd gone into the refuge of the cerebral and analytical. Truth be told, I think all my emotions were firing—even a touch of fear—fear of saying the wrong thing, of not being worthy. What the interviewer couldn't see was that I was using everything God gave me just to keep my mouth in some semblance of contact with my brain, and the only thing I knew for certain was that the prize felt abstract. Unreal. I couldn't relate a million dollars to myself or anything I'd done. I couldn't connect it to my past, my present, or my future.

In my hand was a #10 envelope printed with Pillsbury's blue logo. I didn't look inside, I simply clutched it for the duration of the press conference.

Odd as it may sound, I began to feel distracted by not having gathered up my things in my room. Theoretically, I had already checked out and made myself ready to board a bus for the airport. But I hadn't. My jacket and purse were on the bed. My toothbrush and lipstick were in the bathroom. And even though I'd be going to the airport later, I must have latched on to the obsession of tidying up my belongings as a bridge to Life as I'd known it up until winning the prize.

As the reporters' questions wound down, I was ushered into Pillsbury's pressroom, command central of the entire operation— a secret place, off-limits, but opening right onto the hotel's main lobby. I had walked past the unassuming door for three days and hadn't even noticed the room was there, stuffed with telephones, fax machines, and computers poised for instant communications.

In the relative quiet of that work space, with people efficiently coming in and out and working at temporary desks, I began to bring things into sharper focus. Marlene Johnson introduced me to Robin Waxenberg, a vice president of Stawasz & Partners, Pillsbury's New York public relations firm. Two big wheels. They knew what to do with me. In the nicest possible way, they owned me for the moment, and, in the most comfortable sense, I submitted myself to them.

Timing was critical. Little did I know that all kinds of information—along with the photograph of me in the lucky shirt, along with the winning recipe—had already gone out on the wire, and was already on the Internet.

Time was tight. Marlene, Robin, and I would be flying to Los Angeles together that afternoon, and there was much to attend to before we left, such as me opening a big blue box that contained a huge Waterford crystal bowl—trophy size.

"We figured someday the money will be gone," Marlene said, "but your family might want to have some kind of heirloom as a reminder." A second, smaller blue box contained a walnut stand with a brass plaque. "We'll get your name engraved," Marlene added, "and don't worry. We'll FedEx the bowl out to you." I had never considered how to ship a piece of cut crystal that big. Would light stop dancing on its facets when the lid was taped shut?

I'm nuts about glass. After all, I come from Dale Chihuly territory. Seattle is the center of the recent American art glass resurgence. I had wanted to go to Waterford when I was in Ireland with Karen, but the roads were flooded and we went to Cork instead. I was thrilled with that bowl. It was tangible. Real. Something I could understand. I could fill it with pink camellias, rhododendrons, a dozen lemons.

A pyramid of hotel sandwiches showed up, cut into appealing white-bread triangles, but I couldn't eat. There were too many other things to attend to. The bowl, the plane, Los Angeles, my suitcase, that envelope, my hotel room, where my jacket and purse were still on the bed.

I said I was concerned that I hadn't cleared out of my room. Don't be silly, someone responded. We'll get an assistant to take care of that for you. She thought it was funny I'd have something that trivial on my mind, and—okay—maybe it was odd. But I needed a semblance of reality to cling to. The expiration of a rented room was something I knew how to deal with. Plus, I'm very keen on doing things in order. To me, that errand felt like next on the list. By my standards anyway. And I didn't want some stranger gathering up my ratty cosmetics. It must have come clear that I wouldn't be satisfied until I was excused to take care of that loose end.

I remember the delicious moment alone in the elevator, the calm of entering that room with its unmade bed, of closing the heavy door behind me, just long enough to scoop up my things.

Back in the pressroom, phone interviews had been lined up. I didn't sense it at the time, but these two- and three-minute interviews must certainly have been prearranged and maybe even scheduled in accordance with some complex formula of priority. In the news business, whoever gets the story first is on the top of some kind of special heap.

The telephone was handed to me skillfully as interviews unfolded one by one. If anyone had said at the outset, "We have twenty people lined up to talk to you live on radio shows across the country," I might have gone a bit numb. But Marlene and Robin were pros. They said things like, "Oh, would you mind talking to so-and-so for a minute? He's with such-and-such radio and just wants a quick word." It sounded and felt casual each time, and light enough to put me at ease. The interviewers themselves also put me at ease, congratulating me and asking how it felt to win such a big prize. Most asked what I intended to do with the money. "I have no idea," I answered over and over.

There was Carl to call, too. He would be watching the broadcast, but it was delayed three hours for the West Coast. I probably should have called him while I was on the fourth floor in my unmade room, but I hadn't dared to linger. I wasn't thinking clearly enough to have had the foresight, anyway.

Back in the pressroom they kept urging me to call home, holding out the phone to me, offering to dial my number. The thought of bringing my private life with Carl into contact with that very public scene wasn't something I was ready for. I was at the height of my fluster, and I felt rushed. I'm sure the people in that room had more than a passing interest in hearing how I would break the news. To think of telling Carl such big news in the midst of strangers, though...Would the people listening to my end of the conversation expect me to gush? Should I fake it?

But there was no getting around it. The call needed to be made. At the very least I had to tell him I wouldn't be home as planned.

Ever since we've been married, Carl and I, and Karen, have used two code words to indicate when one of us is in a situation where we can't talk freely. It means the person on the other end should carry the conversation. I didn't think to use our code, but I hoped Carl would do most of the talking if I started out, "Hi. It looks as if we can go ahead and arrange to have that well drilled." I thought it might be enough that Carl was hearing from me at all to give him the idea I'd won, since I'd told him I wouldn't be calling before I got home.

"A well?" he responded.

"At Chiwaukum Creek. A well. What we talked about."

Carl sounded bewildered. He wasn't getting it.

"Don't you remember we agreed to get a well at the Chiwaukum if, you know, if I won?" Never mind that the cabin and the Chiwaukum Valley were still under four feet of snow at that time of year. It would be two months before anyone would be able to get in without a pair of skis.

"You won one of the prizes?" he said. "That's great."

"I won *the* prize," I said. "That's what I'm telling you." I remember specifically trying to speak softly into the phone. I wanted him to get my point without my actually having to be explicit. I couldn't bring myself to use the phrase *grand prize*. I don't know why. My overriding sense was one of embarrassment—with the terminology, and with the feeling of not having earned the award I'd been given.

"You won the million?!"

"Yes."

"You won the grand prize?!" Carl's voice was quivering the way it does when he's about to cry.

"I have to fly to Los Angeles," I said, "so don't go to the airport to pick me up this afternoon."

"Los Angeles?"

"I'll call you again after I know when I'll be coming home. Probably some time tomorrow. They want me to be on some talk show called Rosy O'Donald. Have we ever heard of her?"

"You actually won the million?" By then Carl *was* crying. "Oh, my *God*. A million dollars? You're going to be on *The Rosie O'Donnell Show*??!"

Apparently, he had heard of her.

CHAPTER TWENTY

Toward the end of that phone call, Carl said, "Did you know they don't give you the money all at once?"

"No?"

"It's an annuity."

"Oh."

"I read the rules online a while back," he said. "They'll pay you fifty thousand a year for twenty years."

"Yikes."

By then I had zipped my unopened, blue-printed #10 envelope into the outer pocket of my carry-on bag and stashed the bag in a corner of the pressroom. I hadn't yet wondered what, precisely, was inside the envelope. Maybe a letter? I trusted Pillsbury to make good on the prize but hadn't thought about the details of how. I certainly didn't fantasize holding a check right then and there printed with *Pay to the Order of... in the amount of One Million Dollars.* I guess I had the vague notion that money beyond a certain amount wouldn't be handled by check anyway.

Over and over, Carl saves me from myself, as he did in that phone call. I would not have wanted the women in that room to know I hadn't read the fine print before entering the contest. With Carl coaching me from the sidelines, I could avoid revealing my ignorance. As soon as he told me, I preferred the idea of receiving the prize chunk by chunk and not in a big heap all at once. So daunting either way, but—like the Waterford bowl—fifty thousand a year was comprehensible, whereas a million in my lap? Who, out of an ordinary life, knows what to do with that kind of money?

"I'll call you when we get to L.A." I said to Carl. I was beginning to feel foggy. "Love you."

"I love you, too," he said. "Don't forget that."

TECHNICALLY, I could have left Pillsbury in the lurch with their trip to televisionland and said no thank you. I could have gone home directly without passing Go. But that thought never dawned on me. If Hollywood was part of the package, I was ready, willing, and able. Besides, I'd never been behind the scenes in a television studio.

Our flight from Orlando to Los Angeles was full to the gills, including the Trebek family of four in first class. Alex said something to Marlene as we squeezed toward our seats in coach section, while he gave me only a minimal nod. I reminded myself he probably had a relationship with Marlene from having made arrangements to be at the Bake-Off, but it felt funny not to have some sort of exchange with him.

We hadn't been able to get seats together. Mine was on the aisle, with Robin, the public relations queen, and her bulging briefcase directly behind me. She had looked worried when she realized I didn't know who Rosie O'Donnell was, so, as soon as our plane was airborne, Robin began handing me pages of background information. I imagine Pillsbury would have preferred to award their big prize to someone who didn't hole up in a cabin with kerosene lamps and no running water, someone who would thrill at meeting a famous television star and who would rise to the occasion in a spin of excitement. Luckily, soon as I saw O'Donnell's picture, I was able to dredge up a glimmer of recognition.

"Didn't she play Meg Ryan's friend in *Sleepless in Seattle*?" I asked, as Robin breathed a sigh of relief.

The articles about O'Donnell focused on her reputation as the Queen of Nice and made much of her penchant for junk food, but what Robin stressed was O'Donnell's soft spot for kids.

Robin's briefcase must have also contained a thousand critical phone numbers. Over the drone of the plane's engines, while I dutifully read PR material on the daytime talkmeistress, I could hear Robin using the Airfone in her row of seats. More than once, she tapped my shoulder to ask whether I'd mind talking to this or that reporter. Then she'd hand her phone up to me.

If I leaned into the aisle, the cord was just long enough to reach my ear.

I especially liked my interview with Gregory Roberts from the *Post-Intelligencer*, Seattle's morning paper. No doubt part of the appeal was that I was talking to someone from home. Roberts asked me how it felt to win a million. But at that point, I didn't really know. Everything had been such a rush, and I'd barely had a moment to reflect on any of it, let alone talk it out with Carl or Karen or anyone else important to me. The experience was still encapsulated in the realm of strangers and not linked to my own world in any tangible way.

The reporter knew in advance that I was a writer. I told him that winning the Bake-Off felt good in the same way as having my work accepted for publication.

"Aw, c'mon," he said, "winning a million?"

I suppose he, more than most, would be skeptical; his work was accepted for publication every day. No big deal for him to see his name in print. That's what journalists do. For a fiction writer, however, it takes a lot to sell that first story. And sometimes even more to sell the second one.

It probably would have been easier for both of us if I'd simply said I felt thrilled or ecstatic—or even euphoric—and left it at that. But I was still trying to personalize my response to Roberts. In support of comparing the prize to succeeding as a writer, I said, "Each instance reflects on something that was my own creation. I like the confirmation that someone thought I did something well."

With that, something clicked. Roberts's tone changed; the challenge went out of his voice, and he quit pushing for the stock answers. He seemed to get it that the interview wasn't going to be about my gushing over the impact of money. The rest of our exchange went smoothly, and, in the end, his article was among my favorites of those I saw.

I used to fly a lot for work, but I'd never used a phone on an airplane. I was surprised at the clarity of the connection and by how natural it felt to have a conversation from 35,000 feet.

I probably could have asked Robin to dial into my own number in Seattle and hand me that call, too. I longed to talk more with Carl now that he'd had a few hours to absorb the force of my win. But I wouldn't have any more privacy from the plane than I'd had in Orlando. The women in the pressroom had seen my emotional lock-up on stage and later in the press conference. I couldn't blame them if they'd wanted to listen in, wondering, when does this woman ever let loose?

I felt the same privacy constraints on that flight. Too many people in my midst. At Marlene's suggestion—and with my approval—a flight attendant had already clicked on the PA system and announced that Pillsbury's million-dollar Bake-Off winner was on board. The man in the window seat of my row put two and two together when he heard the announcement and then saw me flipping through Bake-Off material. He seemed nice, but who could blame him if he was inclined to eavesdrop on a freshly minted millionaire talking to her husband. And, sure, I was never going to see this man again, so what would it matter?

But I wasn't fully in my right mind on that flight. No matter how much I might be dying to talk to Carl, I wasn't ready for another cryptic exchange. I wanted a normal conversation, one where we could talk the way we usually talk to each other. Without anyone listening in.

I tried to relax. I dug around for my package of Ak-mak, the Armenian crackers with biblical references on the box that are my travel pantry standby. I offered one to my seatmate by the window, crunched down on one myself, and considered the counterpoint of whole wheat and sesame to the party I'd been indulging in.

When we landed at LAX, I thrilled to see a bank of regular pay phones lining the wall within sight of our baggage carousel. While Robin and Marlene waited for luggage to show up, I peeled off and punched in my credit card and home numbers.

Carl answered on the first ring. "Karen is in labor."

"Ohmygod." My eyes immediately flooded. I didn't care if anyone saw me crying. People at airports cry. "Is she okay?"

"It started at about midnight last night, but they didn't want to wake me. I didn't know until I tried to find her this morning to tell her you'd won. Then I put it together."

"But is she okay?"

"I went to the hospital. They had her walking the hall to try to speed things along."

I could see my handlers at the carousel with our bags lined up. "I'll call again when we get wherever it is we're going," I felt as if I were connected to home via a long tube, now disintegrating and filling with fog. "Love you," I said into the distance and through tears.

"My daughter's in labor," I told Robin. Marlene was off dealing with rental car details. "I'm a mess."

"When we get in the car I'll give you my cell phone. You can talk as long as you want. It'll take a while to get to Century City."

But that conversation, too, felt clipped, coded, and incomplete. Carl, fabulous human being that he is, bore with me and the imperfections of a telephone call from a car. The background noise. The freeway traffic. I wanted normal.

In the luxury of that big, white backseat, Marlene and I began a conversation about what clothes I had with me. I was still in the beige getup I'd put on that morning.

"Well, I have a good pair of jeans in my bag," I said. "And a pair of green cotton pants, pretty wrinkled by now. But maybe we could iron them at the hotel. And I have the silk shirt with the vacation print that I wore to cook in."

"What about shoes?" Robin asked.

"Just these slides I'm wearing. And a pair of patent leather Birkenstocks that used to be my sister's."

"Would it bother you if we tried to find you something new?" Marlene caught my eye in the rearview mirror as she drove. "It's just that some clothes work better for television than others."

I suppose I could have chosen to feel insulted. I could have understood her to be saying I wasn't well enough dressed to represent Pillsbury, that she thought I did, in fact, look hopelessly lumpy in what I was wearing. But Marlene was just so darned nice about suggesting a new outfit, there was no offense to be taken.

We agreed then on a plan to go shopping. In the morning there would be time to launch ourselves onto the shores of a big California mall. There, we'd figure out jointly what one might wear on daytime television to convey all-American cook. Not Birkenstocks, apparently. Marlene and Robin would tactfully spin me around at the door of half a dozen dressing rooms, evaluating the potential of what I'd tried on to model for them. As it would turn out, we would leave retail heaven with a pair of khaki pants and a belt from the Gap, two turtlenecks from Macy's—one royal blue, the other bittersweet orange—a pair of white anklets, and a pair of dressy loafers.

Having Pillsbury take charge of my wardrobe took the heat off me. I so much wanted to please them—to look the way they wanted me to look, to promote the Bake-Off the way they wanted it promoted, to come across the way they wanted me to come across—even if the delicate merino wool of the turtlenecks was going to itch something fierce.

For now, though, in the car, on that freeway, they began coaching me on what to say when my turn came up on the air. Rosie didn't want anything political, I was told. And maybe I should steer my responses toward her soft spot for kids. They told me her son was named Parker. Maybe I could bring him into the conversation. I wasn't sure how fawning over her little boy would tie in with cooking, but in the spirit of the moment I determined to give it a try if at all possible.

CHAPTER TWENTY-ONE

I had been on Pacific time when I was in Florida, but now that I was back on the West Coast, I felt as if the big hand and the little hand were spinning in googly-eyed opposite directions. My body and mind weren't fully connected. With gratitude and relief, I submitted myself to following the trail of gingerbread crumbs my handlers were laying out before me. Meals. Clothes. Scheduling. I put my physical being in trust to Pillsbury.

At the hotel desk, Marlene asked whether I'd want to tuck my cashier's check in the hotel safe. I decided not to. Too much bother and I didn't want anyone to see that I'd forgotten which pocket I zipped the thing into. Or maybe it was in my purse? I wanted a moment in my room to check in with Carl again. We'd been talking in such herky-jerky bits and pieces of conversations,

I still felt we hadn't assimilated anything significant. Even under normal circumstances, we talk a lot. And these were not normal circumstances.

Before we left Orlando Marlene had asked whether I'd like the company to fly Carl down to Los Angeles to see me on the Rosie show. I couldn't imagine anything more appealing than to have Carl at my side as soon as was aeronautically possible. But getting Carl on an airplane bound for California seemed to go against the flow of my getting home to Seattle. More than that Karen was in labor. Granted, she and our son-in-law had made it clear that they were going to want total privacy for the birth. Still, it seemed rational for one of her parents to stick around Seattle. Just in case.

AFTER dinner I indulged in one more call home. No news from the hospital, Carl told me, but he had plenty else to report on.

"The phone has been ringing nonstop," he said.

Early in the day Carl had gone down the street to where our friend Beth works to give her our news in person. "In just those few minutes that I was gone," Carl said, "a reporter from the *P-I* showed up. When he found no one home at our house, he went next door."

"He interviewed Barb?"

"She knew better than to fall for it. Said if he wanted to know what kind of person you are—or cook or housekeeper or whatever—he'll have to wait until he can go direct."

"Barb's a saint."

Then Carl mentioned a name I hadn't heard in a long, long time, the name of a woman I'd met under intense circumstances, someone I cared about but had lost contact with. "Mary DeFelice called," Carl said. "I guess I should have said that to begin with. But this place has my mind in a blender."

"Mary? She knew our number?"

"Well, actually, she called the *Times* and the *Times* called here to ask permission to give her our number."

"Well, of *course*," I said. "I hope you gave it double." I was once again in tears. "But why the *Times*?"

"She wanted to tell them what kind of person Ellie Mathews is. That there's more to you than winning a contest."

Carl is used to hearing me cry when I'm happy, but the long pause while I caught my breath had him asking, "Are you okay?"

"I can't wait to see her," I finally squeaked out.

"The paper wants to do an article on how the two of you met."

The prize, the new baby, and now this, a reunion I thought I'd never have. Too many good things were happening at once.

Ten years before, at the height of our Northwest summer, Carl and I had gone backpacking with another couple into the wilderness of the North Cascades National Park. Our destination the first day was a place called Cottonwood Camp. We had hiked eight miles up and over the spine of Washington State, with one more mile to descend into the Stehekin Valley, when we encountered a search party. Men with two-way radios and safety equipment thumped past us on the trail, and a Park Service helicopter's blades thwacked overhead. Clearly, something was wrong.

Maybe twenty minutes later, after traversing scree and talus above the crash of glacial meltwater, we arrived at Cottonwood, a quiet clearing in deep conifer woods. A woman in her mid thirties paced the soft forest floor. Her backpacker shorts and well-worn boots told me she was a veteran of the wilderness. I liked her right away. Her quick, graceful manner conveyed trust. I was struck by how open and astonishingly calm she was, given the vulnerable circumstances she described. Recently engaged to be married, she and her fiancé had set up their camp the day before, planning to spend a few days soaking up the splendor of the high, jagged peaks and the spicy ponderosa scent of the backcountry. He had gone off climbing that first afternoon while she'd dozed against a sloped granite boulder, but by dinner he hadn't come back. By dark he hadn't come back. Alone in the mountains, she had no choice but to wait, by then unable to sleep. In the tent they'd erected together, she struggled through the night, willing herself not to think the obvious thoughts. That morning she had hiked out to meet the first of two daily buses, asking for someone to radio for help.

That woman was Mary.

Early afternoon found Carl and me sitting with our friends at a picnic table in Cottonwood Camp, also waiting for the search party's outcome. Mary had drifted off. A ranger set down his radio on the table without turning it off. Like Mary, he paced the forest floor, waiting for word. A few staticky minutes later, a radioed voice squawked out the discovery that a man's body had been seen from the air, on the rocks at the base of a snowfield.

It's not that I didn't trust the ranger, but by then, I already felt protective of Mary.

"Ever done this before?" I asked him, meaning was he experienced in delivering news of a death. Not that I was either.

He lifted his government-issue straw hat and ran his hand through short hair. "Maybe you could come with me," he said.

The two of us followed down the little path to where Mary sat by the Stehekin River. We stood silent with her for half a minute or so before confirming what she already feared. The intimacy of those moments had the power of the river.

Mary asked for some time to sit alone on a log. We left her to look deep into moving water, to raise her eyes toward Horseshoe Basin, where her fiancé's broken body lay. When she emerged she explored with the ranger the practicalities of seeing the accident site before recovery, but the ranger discouraged her, given the terrain and the increasing slant of the sun.

Like me, Mary lived in Seattle. Getting home was not going to be easy. We were trapped by the geography we'd both gone there to enjoy. She had followed a different route than Carl and I and our friends. She had reached Cottonwood from the east side of the Cascades by highway and boat and bus. Our car was up a winding dirt road on the western side. For her to retrace her steps required twenty-two rattling miles down a primitive road, a four-hour boat ride down a long, fiordlike lake to the small town of Chelan, where she and her fiancé had parked their car at the boat dock, then on to Seattle, a 180-mile drive.

That's how it would have usually worked. Except the last downlake boat of the day had left.

Carl and I agreed that I would split off from him, our friends, and the remainder of our weekend together. With the help of the Park Service, I chartered a float plane to fly uplake, fetch Mary and me at the head of the lake, and deliver us the fifty-five mile distance back down to her car.

At 3:30 the tiny plane arrived, bucking in the waves at the end of the dock. The pilot leapt out, loaded our gear, and said with something of a snort, "Two people and three backpacks?" as if to suggest we didn't know the proper way to prepare for an outing. Then he looked at our faces, clicked, and said nothing more about the extra pack.

Mary was terrified by small planes. Me, too, especially when flying over deep water, which we'd be doing for a good half hour. But this ride wasn't about me and my phobias. I held Mary's hand for the duration of the flight, each of us squeezing until our knuckles went white.

It felt as natural as gravity itself for me to see Mary home. We had a long drive ahead of us. My purpose was to be someone to talk to. Or not talk to. Whatever felt more supportive. Between silences along the golden hills of central Washington, I learned that she worked in a bank; he drove a city bus. In their off hours they were both musicians, avid folk dancers. He had recently ordered a custom-made accordion. He was a risk taker. She was not, and had just that summer learned how to slip off on her own when his ebullience veered into territory that made her feel unsafe. Like on that mountain. Like on that snowfield.

Days later, I attended the funeral, and weeks later, the memorial service for a man I'd never met. Mary and I kept in close touch. Carl and I invited her to our Christmas party. On his winter break, the ranger who had walked down the path with me that day to deliver the awful news came through Seattle, and the three of us had dinner. Eventually, though, Mary moved; then Carl and I moved. Somehow we lost track of each other. I imagined she might have returned to Massachusetts where her family lived.

But she had not. And now, as a result of having my name in the news, I was to be blessed with a powerful counterpoint to all the fluff and frosting that the Bake-Off had to offer. The thought of reconnecting with this lovely, tender, thoughtful woman brought me back to center. The reporter from the *Seattle Times* wanted to get us together as soon as I returned home.

But when would that be? I'd already agreed to an extra night in Los Angeles for the purpose of doing a morning spot with the NBC affiliate there. That would have me getting home midday on Thursday, but Carl said the Seattle ABC affiliate had scheduled me to come into the studio on Friday. And there was talk of me flying to Nashville on Sunday to do something with one of the cable channels. If I didn't mind.

Before any of that, however, there was *The Rosie O'Donnell*

Show. And Karen to congratulate and care for the minute I arrived home. And Carl to kiss all over for keeping things nailed down in my absence. And my tiny granddaughter to welcome, almost too big an event to think of while in Los Angeles. Like someone in survival mode, I had to direct my energies to putting one step in front of another. That's what would get me home.

Chapter Twenty-two

The phone rang me awake at 7:00 the next morning.

"It's a girl," Carl said.

"We knew *that*, but when?"

"Right after midnight. I didn't want to wake you."

"Poor Karen, in labor so long."

"Brace yourself," Carl said. He paused, choked up. "They named her Loa Emeline."

I choked up, too. My sister had never liked her old-fashioned name, but Karen and she were as close as aunt and niece can be. Like the rest of us, Karen was devastated over Emeline's death. Karen had hinted that she might honor my sister's name. Using it as Loa's middle name seemed perfect.

I blotted my eyes on the hotel sheet and fumbled for the hotel pen and paper beside the bed while Carl rattled off the number for Karen's hospital room.

"When will you become television's darling of the day?" he asked.

"In the afternoon. And get this: they're going to send a *limousine* for us."

I couldn't get through to Karen. A nurse said she and her husband and the baby were all sound asleep. No wonder.

Next my sister Sylvia called. Obviously, she found me through Carl, but she can track down anyone anywhere; she used to be a private investigator for a big-time criminal lawyer, and she's always up on the details. "What's new, if anything?" she asked with a smile. We talked about the baby before getting to the thunder and lightning of the contest.

Then I called a friend to cancel a get-together we'd arranged for that night. I thought I had a pretty good excuse, after all. Other than family, he was the first person from home I talked to, PBO (post-Bake-Off). It felt amazingly normalizing just to yak. Ten minutes of talking to him reset all my dials to their default positions.

For breakfast that morning I ordered oatmeal. That's what I have when I know it's time to slow down. Forget the high-fat griddle goodies, the ooey-gooey cinnamon pastries. Forget the bacon, the hollandaise sauce potential of what the menu had to offer. I needed the stabilizing effect of boiled food.

The limousine arrived midday and slid us easily into NBC territory. Angelica Huston crossed in front of us. We drifted by the studio where the doctor drama *ER* is produced. I pinched myself, a reminder not to let any of this high-profile world go to my head.

The O'Donnell media machine was based in New York, but Team Rosie was fully installed in L.A. for a one-month stint on the West Coast. Not that rare, I guess, for television shows to go flitting around the country to connect with their audiences. From the outside, the building we entered looked like an airplane hangar, but the inside was an oversized warren of trailers and temporary rooms.

Our trailer had my name posted on the door. Inside were fresh flowers, a folded jersey for me to take home, and a small fridge, completely stocked with snacks and drinks. The shirt was thick and chunky, with long sleeves and the show's logo stitched on the front.

"Over here is our greenroom," our greeter said. "You can wait here or in your trailer. Our director will come find you in a few minutes."

The greenroom wasn't green, but that didn't matter. In it were trays of French pastries and fresh fruit and cut-up vegetables. There was a platter of bagels and a mountain of lox, sodas and sparkling waters on ice next to a coffee urn, and a carafe of hot water with every kind of tea, both ordinary and exotic.

A few people scuttled around in whispers at the edge of the room—friends of friends working behind the scenes, I was told. Other guests scheduled for the show that day were Jane Curtin of *Saturday Night Live* fame and the comedian Martin Short, but they were nowhere to be seen. I supposed a real star wouldn't need to vulture around the free croissants. I learned Curtin and Short had the sanctuary of their own trailers anyway.

It was hard to distinguish between staff and general millers-around. People were in and out, most of them dressed in black and carrying clipboards. I had thought I might feel dazzled amid the trappings of fame but I felt more like a distant observer than an actual participant. I love to see the details of what it takes to get things accomplished, like when Carl and I had visited that cattle feedlot in Kennewick, Washington. You can't beat an inside view on work that isn't ordinarily on view.

Marlene and Robin were busy with a woman who was there as my food stylist. "She brought all your ingredients," Marlene said, "so you won't have to do anything but relax. She'll have your dish already made up by the time you get out there. You've seen shows when they do a cooking segment, and how they always pull out the finished dish at the end?"

I'd imagined sitting on the couch and talking with Rosie about my experience at the Bake-Off. It seemed, however, that I'd be doing a cooking demo instead. The singers Steve Lawrence and Eydie Gorme were guest hosting with Rosie for the week. Three of them to one of me.

A man in black found me and said he was assistant director. He explained that someone would take me to makeup. Then I'd get wired for sound. Then I'd have a run-through on the set. He was exceedingly upbeat.

The makeup person had her own trailer. She directed me

to sit in a tall director's chair before a rainbow of powders and creams and eye paints. She didn't wear a lick of color herself and didn't say much except, "Look down, look up. Now to the side, please." At the end she added, "Don't freak out when you look at yourself up close. What you see on camera is never real."

I was moved to another chair in the same trailer, where my hair was brushed, fluffed, teased, and tamed. The stylist asked if I minded a bit of spray before he depressed the nozzle and then went at my head as if putting out a fire.

When I looked at myself in the mirror, I saw a face with only faint hints of familiarity.

There was one question I could count on from just about everyone—including the hair man. "Ever been on television?"

"No."

"Nervous?"

"No."

"Well, don't be. You don't have a thing to worry about."

Meanwhile, the Pillsbury Doughboy had shown up—or, at least, the young woman who'd been hired to climb into the Doughboy suit. I had learned earlier that Pillsbury typically goes through a local talent agency, requesting someone short enough to see through the mesh mouth that's stitched into the white leather of the suit, and tough enough to bear the weight of the backpack fan mechanism that both ventilates and inflates the outfit. The woman they'd found for this gig—a college student—seemed game for just about anything. I liked her. We sat side by side in our trailer. She felt like an ally.

Another man dressed in black, like the assistant director, found me, put his arm across my shoulders, and walked me a few feet. "What's your dish called again?"

I told him.

"Oh. Never mind. Is there a funny story about how you came up with this recipe? Like a cooking disaster?"

"Not really."

"Oh. But did you, like, leap up in the air or fall over when they told you that you'd won?"

"I was too stunned," I admitted.

"Well, whatever. Here's our director. She'll take you for run-through."

Clutching her clipboard tight to her waist like a vital organ trying to be transplanted, the director repeated many of these same questions. It was clear that the show was trying to ferret out a funny goof I might have made on my way to the Bake-Off. I was fully invested in playing by their rules and being a good sport for the sake of this exercise, but I began sensing a disconnect: they wanted comedy. Oh, dear.

Maybe when I get face-to-face with Rosie, I thought, *then we'll be in sync.*

The director with her clipboard was undeniably efficient. "Follow me," she said, leading me through winding, black-painted, beat-up plywood passages, down a few stairs, past black drapes, and out onto the set, where a dozen or more people buzzed purposefully about with huge cameras and cranes. The director must have noticed me looking around expectantly.

"Rosie never does run-through," she said.

The set was big. The classic talk show double throne of host-desk and guest-couch stood off to the side on an elevated stage. The movie *Titanic* was in theaters then, and there was going to be some sort of tie-in ahead of my appearance. Workers were putting together props with a quasi-nautical theme off to the side. The "kitchen" where I'd be "cooking" stood in the middle. I looked up at the audience seats, empty now and dark, and tried to imagine people sitting there. Then I looked down. Black cables as big as anacondas laced the floor. The side of the kitchen island where I'd be facing the audience revealed a clatter of mismatched pans stacked into the cabinet every which way.

The producer followed my glance. "Don't worry about any of that," she said, as she gave the stuff a shove. "You've got your own stylist. She'll have your pans." I went on faith that everything would work out.

Back in my trailer the sound man found me. I tried to make myself into a mannequin while he clipped what looked like a Walkman to the back of my new belt. He tugged on it, and me, a couple of times to make sure we were securely attached, then stuffed excess wire into the pocket of my new khakis, a stranger with his hand in my pants. He threaded the end of the wire between my new turtleneck—the bittersweet orange one—and the bib of my blue Pillsbury apron. I had the apron on inside out in accordance with instructions; word had come that *The Rosie O'Donnell Show* didn't want the company's name on display. But who were we kidding? We would be saying the name of the company every time we said the name of the contest. At last, the sound man clipped a spider-sized microphone to the top of my apron and said I was done.

The whole place was dotted with television monitors: in the greenroom, in our trailer. They were like bright jewels among the tattered black plywood of the real Hollywood. The show was produced "live to tape," meaning they recorded it one day and—barring any serious glitches—aired it the next. As soon as taping began, I turned my attention to watching the top of the show. Sure enough, there were Steve 'n' Eydie belting it out with Rosie. Each was dressed in a sailor suit and equipped with a canoe paddle to be dipped rhythmically in front of cardboard waves breaking in geometric curlicues along the Plimsoll line of a plywood hull identified as the *Titanic*.

About half an hour into the show, it was my turn. Marlene, Robin, and our food stylist—another Marlene—followed along to watch from the wings. They gave me thumbs-ups and said, "Break a leg." The floor director checked that the sound equipment on my belt hadn't dislodged. "And what are we going to remember to do?" she asked me.

"Uh—"

"We're going to smile. Even if you drop a pan on your toe, huh? Remember to look at the camera. You don't have to look at Rosie to make people think you're having a conversation." Then, as an afterthought, "And nothing political, okay?"

Everything looked and felt different from our run-through.

Audience seats were full of warm bodies, their presence creating a faint background rustle. Lighting was on full force now. But it was too late to think about any of that. Worse than taking final exams. This was live. Or nearly so.

THE cooking island where we stood was about the size of a burial vault, not quite big enough for the four of us to crowd behind. On the work surface sat a giant basket overflowing with potato chips, a platter loaded with maybe four dozen chocolate chip cookies, a display of Old El Paso Salsa, an arrangement of Asiatic lilies, my ingredients, a display of Pillsbury refrigerated cookie dough, and another heap of baked cookies.

Food stylist Marlene Brown had supplied the set with two cooking spoons, one Teflon, the other wooden, presumably for me to have a choice. From the start, Rosie took command of one, Eydie the other. Throughout, Rosie variously twirled the long-handled wooden spoon, pointed with it, and banged it on the counter for emphasis. Steve, on the far end, fought for territory. I was sandwiched between Rosie and Eydie, at the geographic sweet spot of our foursome, in front of the single burner where the cooking action would be.

Steve introduced me. I could see his script scrolling on the little blue teleprompter screen, below the camera trained on his face.

Then Rosie's teleprompter rolled. "When they called to tell you you'd won, what'd you think?" she said.

Oops, that's not how the contest had worked. But the cameras were rolling. I stumbled out an answer.

"So, Ellie, are you a really good cook?" Rosie asked.

Yes would have sounded like bragging; *no* would not be honest. "I'm an adequate cook," I said, trying as hard as I could to figure out the right answer.

Television minutes are like dog years. One rotation of the thin red hand on the studio clock counts for more than sixty seconds in an ordinary life. In my brief appearance that day, my overly earnest replies were barely audible above the interruptions and vies for attention. Questions directed to me were answered by others.

Somewhere in there I began to dump my ingredients into the waiting pan. When it came time to add the cumin, Rosie pretended to misunderstand me. She said to the camera, "Human? Ellie, don't scare me. For a minute I thought you were going to put a human in there."

I continued with my ingredients, not quite sure that I was doing the right thing. What could I do but soldier on? Eydie put the chicken in the pan; Rosie did the stirring. It seemed they could have done the segment without me.

Rosie quickly lost interest in the cooking. Apropos of nothing she broke open one of the tubes of cookie dough from the display.

"Ever had this?" she asked me.

I didn't honestly know if I had or hadn't eaten Pillsbury cookies. Likely at a potluck or a friends' house. It seemed prudent to say, "Of course."

"D'ya ever eat it raw?"

"I never have," I said. I thought that would satisfy her, but she jabbed a wad of the stuff within an inch of my face.

"Have a taste."

She's joking, right? I laughed as if to say *are you kidding*. "No," I said, turning away.

But she was not joking. "C'mon. Have a taste." She shoved the stuff at me.

I don't like the trend toward gummy, undercooked cookies, let alone the idea of eating raw dough. But it seemed expedient to play along, so I accepted the glob into my mouth.

"It's good, huh?" Rosie insisted.

Again, expediency ruled my response. I looked directly at the camera while declaring for the nation to hear, "It's delicious."

But that wasn't enough. Steve was her next victim. Of the three hundred and nineteen seconds of the segment, twenty-seven of those were dedicated to Rosie chasing Steve around the set aiming a second glob at him saying, "Don't make me hurt you," and "You *will* eat this."

We never did go through the ingredients list of my recipe, let alone the preparation steps, although I did get a chance to say Old El Paso without interruption. Finally, it was time for me to pull out the finished dish that Marlene Brown, the stylist, had arranged and placed ahead of time on the shelf below the counter. I had completely yielded my place in the line-up by then and had ended up standing half a step—or a full step—behind the three hosts. I placed my hands gently on the width of Eydie's hips and asked her to step aside a tiny bit to make room for the platter I was meant to lift up for the camera.

Rosie interpreted for me. "Get the hell out of the way, Eydie, is what she means."

But that is not what I'd meant.

Then Rosie shifted gears. "Y'know we have a special guest who wanted to come and congratulate you, Ellie."

"Who's that?" I said, my brain leaping to Carl: they'd flown him down after all! My focus darted to the wings, the audience. Where would he be emerging?

"Take a look. C'mon out here, surprise guest!"

A curtain opened, and out lumbered the Pillsbury Dough-boy. Not Carl at all. And not a surprise, either. But the woman inside all that white leather inhabited a world I understood. With more sincerity than was rational, I opened my arms wide to embrace the character's comforting girth. Someone from my team had come onstage to rescue me.

It was over. I had at one point mentioned her son by name, as I'd been coached, but I'd made the comment in a normal voice, which disappeared into the chaos around me. If I'd known from the start that my appearance on the show was meant to be a joke, I'd have done it differently from the start. If I'd ever watched the show and gotten a sense of its culture...If there had been fewer of us on stage trying to take command of that one little frying pan...I might not have felt that I had botched it.

CHAPTER TWENTY-THREE

The two Marlenes had worked together before, and we'd be with Marlene Brown the next day to tape the local NBC spot. Ms. Brown was a professional recipe developer as well as a food stylist, and I felt rather in awe of being in the realm of someone who invents and presents food for a living. As a collector of experiences, I was getting more than my fair share in a very short space of time.

Our threesome—Marlene Johnson, Robin the PR queen, and I—arrived for the taping fresh from checking out of the hotel. Marlene Brown worked out of her Glendale home, a big sprawling house with walls spacious enough to display the fruits of her labor: awards, framed magazine covers, feature pages, and photographs, all showing her work. Her salads were more beautiful than bridal bouquets, and the desserts! The quintessence of raspberries nestled into chocolate, with trefoils of mint leaves staking their claim to creamy summits. This woman knew how to garnish.

The ingredients for Salsa Couscous Chicken were already set up in her enormous kitchen—including an assortment of greenery for the platter. No longer constrained by my failure to call for a garnish at the contest, I was now free to use parsley to my heart's content, flat or curly. Marlene had both on hand, although, actually, I wasn't going to be the one in charge of arranging the finished dish. That's the beauty of working with a food stylist. My role would be to dump a few premeasured ingredients into a waiting pan and stir them around while tossing off snappy replies to whatever questions came at me. Afterward, the camera would cut to what the dish looked like in its completion.

Through the window I saw Jim Giggans, journalist with KNBC-TV, pacing smartly up the walk. His cameraman followed, and, because it was Take-Your-Daughter-to-Work Day, his darling six-year-old trailed after. There were eight of us in that open, California kitchen, and it felt like a group of old friends gathering for a casual dinner. Except it was morning, and there was no chummy clink of wineglasses. Although Marlene did welcome us with offers of tea, coffee, and juice.

Taping a spot that is going to be edited is different from taping a talk show, I learned. The camera rolled lazily as I fooled around chopping, stirring, and responding to Giggans's questions. A couple of times we even backed up and repeated something for a second take, or the cameraman asked me to repeat a cooking step so he could try it from a different angle. His yards and yards of tape would be taken back to the studio, where someone would delete glitches, cut in other images and video, and add voice-overs. I hoped everyone would look and sound good by the time the spot aired that evening on the news hour.

Giggans had done his homework and had a good enough grasp of the inner workings of the Bake-Off to ask me relevant questions, so I never felt flat-footed or backed into a corner. I liked him for his easy matter-of-factness. I liked how he talked to his daughter. I felt completely at ease in the company of those people that morning. If Marlene Brown had invited me to stay and apprentice with her for the day, I'd have been more than happy to sign on. Except for the fact that my next stop was LAX. As soon as we were finished in her kitchen, I'd be heading home.

My flight to Seattle blessed me with two and a half hours of do-nothing time when I could begin to gain some perspective on the events of the week. Taking advantage of my locked and upright position, I closed my eyes and let the drone of the jet's engines help me unjumble my thoughts. Karen and the baby were foremost, and on that front I had nothing to figure out except how not to go crazy with joy. And the anticipation of reconnecting with Mary. No ambiguity there.

But the hoopla felt like a blur. What did any of it mean except having had the courage to try and the luck to succeed? I wondered what would be expected of me now. I worried that friends might invite Carl and me to dinner parties less often, assuming I was suddenly too much of a foodie to eat casually prepared meals.

And the money. When I'd been growing up in the fifties, a million dollars was an amount almost beyond comprehension. I remembered cartoons of men in suits lighting cigars with dollar bills and jokes about oil-rich Texans buying new Cadillacs when the gas tanks in their first ones ran dry. That was my school-girl image of wealth. But now I was an adult living in a house we owned free and clear. Carl and I had savings. Lack of money wasn't holding us up from doing the things we wanted to do, or from having what we wanted to have.

I think that people watching a stroke of good luck like mine often yearn to see the money used to rescue the recipient, or buy her something she desperately needs, like on that fifties television game show *Queen for a Day*, where women would describe hardships and mishaps in hopes of being voted the most deserving. Three contestants would vie for the shiny new washing machine or a bus ticket to Toledo to see a long-lost brother or whatever else would dig them out of their particular jam.

I wasn't in a jam. Still, I loved the fact of winning. Reminding myself to attribute the win more to chance than skill, I held out hope that a little tiny part of the award had something to do with me.

IN addition to refinishing the oak floorboards on our second-story landing while I'd been away, Carl had been passing out virtual cigars, along with updates on Karen's progress with Loa Emeline and their homecoming from the hospital. Add to this the task of managing about a thousand calls coming into our house the minute my name hit the airwaves, and any ordinary man would have been a frazzle by the time he greeted me at Sea-Tac Arrivals. But Carl is no ordinary man.

"I went ahead and committed you to do the noon news at KOMO tomorrow. I hope you don't mind," he said as he merged us into the northbound lanes of I-5. "But get this: Seattle is pretty much sold out of salsa."

"You're kidding," I said. It was early afternoon Thursday, only two days since the awards show. "People are making the stuff already?"

"You'd better believe it. As soon as I knew yesterday you'd be doing a demo, I hotfooted it down to Safeway, but I was too late. Nothing but dust on the Old El Paso shelf, so I went to the big QFC on Broadway. No dice. Then I began calling around. Sold out everywhere. And it's not as if Pillsbury would want you to substitute Brand X. Anyway, I called Minneapolis and they're overnighting you some."

"They're FedExing *salsa*?"

"I went ahead and asked for a case of it. Figured why not. Half mild; half medium. And we'd better find you some couscous this afternoon before it's too late."

"Okay, fine," I laughed. "But nothing salsa until I see Karen. And I'd love for things to feel normal for at least part of the afternoon."

Late February in western Washington often has a week of warm spring weather when outside turns almost green enough to turn your retinas into pinwheels. Karen lived eight blocks from our house. We walked over there, which felt blessedly normal. I was back home at last. It seemed as if I'd been away for at least a year, clanking around in a parallel universe.

Karen and company had come home midmorning. She had kissed her husband good-bye and sent him on his way to a day at the office. Her labor had been long, but she'd managed without drugs of any kind. That left her clear-eyed and amazingly perky, considering. Carl and I let ourselves in. She lay on her couch beneath a soft throw, with the television remote at hand. I could hardly believe how natural she looked as a mother.

"I'm not missing you on *Rosie* for all the world," she said. The show was about twenty minutes away.

But television was the furthest thing from my mind. Tucked into the crook of Karen's arm was the most delicate new girl imaginable. I barely dared to look at her, so tiny and perfect. And Karen so serene. After months of hoping and holding our breaths, of watching her grow inside Karen's body, there she was. This new baby. Named for my sister.

Carl and I both choked up immediately. I couldn't believe it, but Karen went digging for Hollywood gossip right away. She pointed her remote toward the TV.

"Karen! It's only quarter to four," I said. "And when the show does come on, it'll be a ton of other people ahead of me. Like half an hour of fooling around."

"That's okay. I've never seen my mother on television before."

"And I've never seen you as a mother before," I said.

"We have the VCR set up at home; we're taping it," Carl said. "We can watch it later."

"Forget Rosie," I said. "Let's look at this small girl here. And you."

Never mind my protestations, the television came on. There were Steve and Eydie clowning around in their sailor suits. There was Rosie O'Donnell paddling along on the cardboard waves, and, actually, it was kind of fun, the three of us like that in private—the four of us if you count Loa, but she was asleep.

I wouldn't say any of us watched the show very carefully, but half an hour into it, my segment came up.

"Whose clothes are those?" Karen asked.

"Pillsbury took me shopping."

"Did you want your hair like that? Were you nervous? What was Rosie like off camera? Did they ask for your autograph? Your recipe?"

"Everyone in the audience got a copy of the Bake-Off cookbook," Carl said. He already knew most of the answers to Karen's questions, so I let him fill in. Anyway, I was busy. Loa had opened her eyes. She looked at me. At least, it looked as if she was looking at me. I gathered the baby onto my lap, touched her fingers. They were no bigger than matchsticks. I touched her nose, her fuzz of hair. All other events of that week slipped below the horizon. All I could think of was the first time I'd held Karen. And now this—my daughter's daughter—like daughter-squared, an exponential increase of what it means to live a life.

Chapter Twenty-four

I have a confession to make. When I present something I've cooked, I tend to apologize.

I usually begin meal preparation chronically optimistic about what I can accomplish—with the ingredients I've chosen or the recipes I've found, you name it. But by the time I get a meal to the table, my confidence has leaked away. I become painfully aware that I've cut corners, been impatient, was too practical to use the three different vinegars that were called for. I fret about my aversion to huge quantities of butter and oil or the fact that I skipped a fussy step such as straining the sauce or peeling the asparagus. Maybe I didn't want to dirty another measuring cup so I slurped out an amount directly from the jar into the pan, hoping I had a sense of what half a cup or a third of a cup should look like. Maybe I substituted lime for lemon if limes were on special that week. So I get something to the table and my cumulative shortcuts and shortcomings hit me. By then it's too late to do anything corrective, so it's not unusual for me to say, "This might not be very good." The words just slip out. A blanket disclaimer. My loss of faith.

It's ironic, since, although I don't cook fancy, I do cook often. And I'm pretty good with peasant food—beans and rice, long-simmering soups made with real bones, casseroles, hearty stews, whole-grain breads. Friends keep coming back. There is always something to eat at our house.

But there is that disclaimer that I can't quite squelch. I even go so far as to mutter on occasion, "I hope this won't be awful." So when Carl told our friend Beth about my win, she went to work on a huge banner, cutting out letters from magazine food pictures and gluing them in place to read, "This might be VERY good." She outlined the word *very* in gold and glitter and posted the banner above the door to our house for all the world to see.

I carefully folded Beth's banner and brought it inside. It was time to go through some of the mail and messages that had begun to stack up. The flood of attention was beyond my imagination. People I barely knew had reached out with congratulations. Neighbors of cousins of my sister's old boyfriends (and other such intimates) began to emerge from the woodwork, with their stories of how they heard my news. The amount of attention was such a drama that I began to wonder: Is there some characteristic innate to our species that has us all inclined to reach out toward a winner? Do we, as homo sapiens, instinctively try to connect with the person at the top of the heap? As if a spangle of stardust might transfer. Or like rubbing the Buddha's tummy.

But before I could respond to anyone's congratulations, to assure them the stardust had been only momentary—if at all—I had another television appearance to prepare for. I would hardly say I'd become a pro at on-air cooking, but I knew my participation on Friday's noon news would be a disaster if I didn't plan ahead. Winging it is one thing; blowing it is another. Carl kept reminding me that my recipe's key ingredients were in short supply on store shelves and that we'd better get on the stick. It would hardly do for me to show up at the studio with a ratty old box of currants from the back of my own pantry, or a beat-up jar of honey, crystallized at the bottom.

Together, Carl and I went to the biggest, baddest supermarket around. Sure enough, the few critical shelves were black holes of low stock. Aware that those vacancies were the direct result of a force I'd created, I felt strangely anonymous in the face of them. Both of the Seattle newspapers had featured my recipe on the front page of their food section the day before. Had people really read those articles and made a beeline to the market that very day?

It turns out that they had. In 1954, when Dorothy Koteen's Open Sesame Pie was announced as the grand prize winner in the fifth Bake-Off, there was a rush on sesame seeds. Similarly, Ella Helfrich put Bundt cakes on the map in 1966 by winning second place in the seventeenth Bake-Off. No sooner did her ingenious recipe for the self-frosting Tunnel of Fudge Cake hit the news than thousands of American cooks went scrambling for the then-exotic pans. NordicWare shifted into overdrive stamping the things out to meet the overnight demand. Subsequently, Pillsbury went into cahoots with NordicWare and introduced a line of cake mixes specifically formulated for those fluted tube pans.

Had I created a blip in couscous sales? Yikes. At the store, Carl groped around to the absolute back of the shelf for the one remaining box, and only by asking the stock clerk to check in the back did I locate a package of currants. Then I tanked up on chicken thighs at the meat counter. And parsley from the produce section. The Thick 'n Chunky airlift from Pillsbury Central would arrive the following morning. By the skin of my teeth, I was all set.

At the station, I learned that meteorologist Todd Johnson delivered restaurant and food reviews every Friday as part of the station's noon broadcast. He ushered me to a somewhat tattered kitchen set, where I arranged my stuff. The routine was the same as in Los Angeles: show the ingredients going into the pan, then bring out the finished dish while trying to keep up an entertaining patter. All this in the space of a few short minutes. Standing with Todd under the studio lights, I was mesmerized by his teeth. Very white. Very straight.

Without passing Go, I took my leftovers from the studio and delivered them to Karen. She had yet to taste her mother's Salsa Couscous Chicken. More than that, though, she could use a catered meal. Next, I rushed home to meet yet another television crew, although this one didn't ask me to cook. For the second time that day I set up the vignette of my ingredients—but this time in the privacy of my kitchen. The cameraman panned and zoomed before Carl and I sat in our dining room for a relaxed Q&A with a very nice reporter, all of which compressed down to one minute and eight seconds on the newscast that night. Even weirder than watching myself on *Rosie* was watching myself against the backdrop of the Van Luit wallpaper in my own dining room.

Television was not the biggest thing on my mind, however—despite the fact that Marlene Johnson seemed to be brewing up another trip for me, this time to Nashville. I was focused instead on the *Seattle Times*, which had scheduled an interview with me for Saturday morning. Mary DeFelice, her husband, a photographer, and a human-interest columnist would be coming to the house.

Meanwhile, I was in desperate need of a haircut. I had intended to get myself tidied up in advance of the Bake-Off, but had been sidelined by the pneumonia that had me bed-bound up until the moment I boarded the plane for Orlando. My regular place takes forever to get an appointment, and I didn't have forever. I reserved a spot at an expensive salon that I'd never been to.

If I really was going to fly to Nashville on Sunday, I would need a new raincoat. Having been greatly influenced by Robin Waxenberg's spiffy, efficient clothes, I'd become obsessed with the inadequacies of my flannel-shirt wardrobe. Robin had just the right gabardine coat, just the right low-heeled shoes, just the right everything. Well, of course she did; she was a vice president at a New York PR firm. Still, I couldn't get out of my mind the possibility of looking like Robin. The sudden *necessity* of looking like her.

Carl could be a front-runner for the Husband of the Year Award. He drove me to the downtown Nordstrom. Nordstrom began in Seattle and, to some, represents the center of our retail universe. But even Nordstrom, with its Northwest origins and its flagship home in the city famous for drizzle, follows the merchandising scheme of selling goods for the upcoming season. At the end of February, they were essentially sold out of winter wear.

In something of a panic, I paid too much for a coat that fit well enough but not well. I'd gone against the wisdom of that famous old Quaker, Henry David Thoreau, when he said, "Beware of all enterprises that [seem to] require new clothes."

At home the next morning, I examined the coat in the light of day. For something brand-new I didn't think the hem should be coming apart. Still obsessing over what to wear to Nashville, I restored the coat to its bag and placed it by the door. Nordstrom is famous for its liberal return policy. I could take the coat back after dinner when I would be going downtown for my hair appointment, where I would want to dish with the stylist about where I'd been, where I was going, and which channel to watch to see her own work, come Monday. I would hold off on that chitchat, though. I was already sensing the catch in telling someone I'd just won a huge money prize.

After all, what kind of tip would she expect?

Chapter Twenty-five

Erik Lacitis, who had interviewed me when I competed in the National Beef Cook-Off, had been a Lifestyle columnist with the *Seattle Times* for a couple of decades, known for his offbeat human interest stories. He'd arranged to interview Mary and me around ten Saturday morning.

Mary and her husband were the first to come up the walk. Through the beveled glass of our heavy front door, she delivered one of her signature full-body smiles. I couldn't welcome her fast enough. In she burst, with hugs all around. Carl and I even embraced her husband, Dave, though we had not met him until that moment. Before he even had his coat off, I could see that this compactly built man exhibited Mary's same trust and openness and wit.

Then Lacitis rang the bell, with his photographer close behind. Everyone's energy level made it feel like more than six of us bunched up in our front hall. I'm not sure why we ended up in the dining room. Maybe I sensed Mr. Lacitis would want to spread out his notes on our big, cherry table.

After introductions were made, I deferred to Mary, letting her relay the details of how we had met. Clearly, the delicacy of the story should be hers to tell. I had been merely out for a walk in the woods on July 21, 1988. She'd been the one with an altered life. But now, never having heard my version of how events had unfolded that day, and with the healing power of time, she was curious. We ended up telling the story together.

Mary began. "My fiancé and I took the four-hour boat up to Stehekin in the North Cascades National Park. Then we took the Park Service bus up the valley to Cottonwood Camp."

I said, "Our friends and Carl and I hiked in from the other direction the next day."

"We planned to camp there for three days, beside the Stehekin River."

"It's nine miles up and over. We had to reach Cottonwood in time for the bus to go down the valley."

"—Our second day there we went up toward Horseshoe Basin."

"—Right below the junction we encountered a search party."

"All afternoon he didn't come back—"

"We knew something was wrong."

"By dinner time I was worried—"

"—We got to Cottonwood Camp, where the trail widens to a dirt road."

"I had to wait out the night in the tent. There wasn't anyone for miles."

"We met Mary at about noon—"

"They came into Cottonwood; it's a big clearing where the bus turns around."

"—She had reported him missing first thing that morning."

"I have this image of sitting with Ellie and her friends at a picnic table."

"Mary was calm in that way some people get when there's a crisis—"

"—After a while someone said maybe I should begin packing up."

"Mary had gone to her tent. We were all waiting for word from the search party. The ranger left his two-way radio—"

"—he and Ellie came toward me—"

"I felt protective of Mary—"

"The ranger—"

"—the river."

Mr. Lacitis asked very few questions. He just took it all in as Mary and I alternated our tumble of details. After an hour or so Mary turned to me and said, "What you did, it really kind of saved my life."

And now she was saving a distinct part of my life in an entirely different way. As if taking me by the hand she was helping to guide me gently back to the Known Universe. The gap of time during which she'd been lost to me evaporated in a matter of minutes. The trust and affection that define friendship invited me into the relaxation of her presence. During the spin of Orlando and L.A., I'd lost some of my sense of true north. Reconnecting with Mary was like finding a compass. And an altimeter. And a clinometer. I was beginning to remember which way was up.

Never once did the interview veer into Bake-Off territory. It wasn't relevant. If only the people at Pillsbury could know what they'd brought me home to.

Mr. Lacitis closed his notebook. He had the details, the outline, the who's who, the sequence of events. All the while, Dave and Carl had listened but not interjected. Now it was time for the photographer to go to work. He wanted Carl in the frame. After all, Carl had helped Mary every bit as much as I did that day, folding and stuffing the camping equipment of a man he'd never meet. Then the mosquito of a float plane had opened itself up to us and carried Mary and me down Lake Chelan and into the hard reality of her grief.

Rising from our dining table, everyone agreed the picture for the *Seattle Times* should be an outdoor shot, since our connection had begun in the woods. The six of us walked the half block to Seattle's Volunteer Park. After a week of cameras aimed at me, this felt different. The smile I directed toward the lens came without hesitation. On this ground, I felt as if I knew what I was doing. And why. All of us were smiling, Mary with her long, dark hair caught by the breeze, Carl in his jeans and sweater, and me in the same cotton coat I'd worn in Orlando. It hadn't been warm enough then, prior to the tornado, but it was fine now, on that bright February day.

Before he left, Mr. Lacitis offered something of a rarity in my experience with journalists: he asked whether I'd like to review the story he'd be writing before submitting it to his editor in a couple of days. Pillsbury had firmed up the proposed trip to Tennessee and I'd agreed to it, so I'd be leaving Seattle the next day for a taping at the Nashville Network cable channel. Somewhere within those few days, I'd hook up with Mr. Lacitis by phone or fax, in case he had any wrinkles in the article that I thought could use smoothing out.

Mary and Dave lingered. Under other circumstances I'd have begged them to stay for a longer visit. Maybe an impromptu lunch. Maybe a game of Scrabble. A return to the park or a walk around the neighborhood. But the phone was constantly ringing, and I was distracted by travel details, and the hope of getting one more peek at Loa Emeline before taking off again. We said good-bye on the promise of another get-together. Soon.

As it was, Carl and I had not had nearly enough time together, just the two of us, to sort things through. Our lives had flipped into the spin cycle, but it seemed the wash wasn't getting wrung out. What better way to come back to Earth after the heady realm of money and media and the intensity of a resurrected friendship than to attend a Quaker meeting for worship? If there was ever a time I might benefit from contemplating my place in the world, that Sunday was one.

University Friends Meeting in Seattle generally finds about eighty people gathering in a tiered circle of silent meditation for its eleven o'clock hour of worship. At the end, it's customary to invite introductions. That's also a time for members who have experienced change in their lives to stand and say a few words. I wanted to announce the birth of our granddaughter to our religious community.

Carl stood with me while I gave the particulars about Karen and Loa. Karen had been connected off and on to that spiritual home since she was a child herself, and now she was a mother.

Carl and I sat down, and one of the other members blurted across the circle, "Don't you have something else to announce?"

"Not today," I said. To me, in that setting, Loa's entry into the world overshadowed my doings with Pillsbury. But my Bake-Off win was announced for me. It was my first lesson that my experience wasn't solely *my* experience. There had been a ripple effect. Already, people who knew me, or knew someone who knew me, felt that they had stories about where they'd been standing when they heard the news, or what they'd eaten at my house once upon a time. Other people wanted to ride along on the fun, too. I can't say I blame them. It's heady stuff, winning such a grand prize.

We ducked out on the social hour. I wasn't quite ready to put my win into a Quaker context. Besides, I had to get ready to fly to Nashville.

CHAPTER TWENTY-SIX

In the language of television, my purpose in Tennessee was to create another "dump and stir" segment, where a food stylist would arrange my premeasured ingredients before I entered the kitchenlike set. I'd place everything sequentially in a pan while trying to craft intelligent responses to the hosts' interview questions. I'd reach under the counter for the platter the stylist had tucked there to show what the finished dish looked like. Then the hosts would dare to take a sample bite and say *Mmm*. I hoped.

The show was *Crook & Chase*, hosted by Lorianne Crook and Charlie Chase. I had never heard of them, but that didn't mean much. Carl and I didn't subscribe to a cable service for television; I'd never heard of the Nashville Network. I assumed the format would be something akin to the *Rosie* show. I put my trust in Pillsbury and its PR firm to which Robin Waxenberg was attached (she of the impeccable wardrobe). Robin couldn't make it to Tennessee. Her associate met me at the hotel in Nashville. In the morning she and I found our way to the television studio together. There we met the stylist whom Pillsbury had engaged and another diminutive college student hired to wear the eight-foot Doughboy getup shipped from Minneapolis.

If a television show can have a personality behind the scenes, *Crook & Chase* had a winning one. Everything about their operation felt welcoming and human, beginning with hair and makeup.

I'm sure the makeup woman could tell at a glance I wasn't the turquoise eye shadow type, because she started out with, "Are you comfortable wearing a little color on your lips?"

Such a natural inquiry might not seem significant, but think of someone painting your face without first getting a feel for how you see yourself. It happens. I appreciated a chance to participate. I was spared the big hair of the overdone. Not that it couldn't have been an option. The country music singer ahead of me on the show sported a pile of orange curls that defied the laws of physics, and the singer seemed quite at home with that arrangement. It matched her bubbly, outgoing personality to a T.

During my prep time backstage, each of the hosts made a point of finding me and thanking me profusely for coming all the way from Seattle to do their show.

After a couple of hours' waiting, my on-air moment arrived.

My two worries about being in front of the camera were as before: would I have a post-pneumonia coughing fit and would I forget the name of my dish, so generic, so utilitarian? I didn't want to embarrass Pillsbury. An assistant discreetly taped my recipe and its name to the counter where I would be standing. A cheat sheet. Right before my cue to go on, someone produced a menthol drop for me to suck on. I loved all those people and how nicely they were taking care of me!

Well. There was one teeny, little glitch. The hosts introduced the nature of the contest to their live audience and viewers at home. Then after a gracious introduction, the first question Lorianne asked was, "What are you going to do with the money?"

I had asked not to be asked that, because I wasn't ready with an answer. I didn't have a clue. I wasn't a week into having received the prize, and most of that week, it seemed, had been spent aboard airplanes and in television studios. I hadn't had a moment to think about my financial life. Still, it's natural to wonder what a million dollars means to someone.

I stumbled out, "I hope to use the money responsibly," the politest way I knew to say I didn't have an entertaining reply. Mercifully, the Doughboy had her cue at just that moment—except that she was supposed to enter the set from the opposite side, where there was a step to descend. The director had failed to factor that in. Once suited up, anyone inhabiting that heavy leather rig can barely see, much less navigate up or down stairs. The Doughboy hesitated. Charlie and Lorianne basically had to lift the poor woman and her inflated white costume onto the set. I welcomed Pillsbury's mascot into the bright lights of the mini-kitchen. What's not to like about the Doughboy? Besides, there was a person in there. I'd spent most of an hour backstage talking to her.

This may have been a dump-and-stir format, but the show went all out to create a realistic cooking demonstration. In addition to country music, both of the hosts had experience with food-related broadcasts. He asked, "What is couscous?" and she asked "Did you experiment a lot when coming up with this recipe?" These were questions I knew how to answer.

When Lorianne wanted to know, "Why did you use thighs instead of boneless, skinless chicken breasts?" that was easy: I like thighs better, which is what I said. For some reason, she and Charlie thought that was hilarious, which I didn't fully understand. It was my recipe, after all.

I slapped a chicken thigh on each of two paper plates for host sampling. The set was stocked with plastic forks but no knives. Charlie and Lorianne hesitated at the thought of going at their hunks of chicken caveman style, but the next logical step was for them to try the stuff. Fortunately, they were pros at keeping the show moving smoothly. It's the sort of television moment you'd never notice if you weren't up close and personal. As if they were used to attacking whole chicken thighs with flimsy plastic forks, they each worried off their obligatory little test bites, took a taste, and gave the requisite *Mmm*'s. Then the flavors seemed to hit Lorianne for real and she gave a second—almost involuntary—*MMM*. This time with feeling.

At the airport later, while waiting for my flight out of

Nashville, I put in a call to Mr. Lacitis from a pay phone. He had faxed me his article so I could check it before the paper ran it the next day. I expected to find a few kinks in the story, something that might need untangling, but he had handled the material with mastery, honoring the profoundly human side of strangers helping strangers. Talking to him, I felt as if I were home already.

I didn't know from reading that faxed copy in the airport that the photograph accompanying the article would run four columns wide in full color above the fold. Nor did I know I would be on the cover of the section. For the second time in less than a week, I looked out at myself from the front page of the paper's lifestyle section.

SIX or seven days later, *Crook & Chase* sent me a videotape of the show I'd been on. They had signed the slipcase like a greeting card. Lorianne's graceful script said, "Now *that* is some million dollar chicken!!" and Charlie's said, "Enjoy your good fortune!" Members of their crew wrote "Yummy recipe," and "Enjoy your million and your new grandbaby."

For weeks, messages like that came at me from all directions. Our mailbox burst with cards and letters, not only in response to the Bake-Off news, but on the Lacitis article in the *Seattle Times* and on my becoming a grandmother.

The parents of the medical resident who rented a room from us sent a card. My sister Sylvia's former boyfriend's parents wrote from Illinois that they had already bragged to their friends that

I had once cooked for them. I heard from editors I'd worked with, and from the Meal Solutions Merchandiser at Kroger Food Stores, who offered me a free ticket to any of their cooking classes, should I happen to find myself in Atlanta, Georgia. Several Bake-Off finalists wrote to me, too. One, Florence Neavoll, from Salem, Oregon, signed herself as "Range 99."

Tim Troendle, who had shared my table at the Planet Hollywood bash in Orlando, sent a note saying that the grand prize winner from 1996 had also been assigned to range 37, the same as me. That sounded positively cosmic; apparently, lightning does strike twice.

I was impressed by the number of people who had lost out to me in the prize department but who sent heartfelt congratulations. I guess I had winner's guilt. I imagined that other contestants had worked harder, practiced recipes longer. Not only did Tim go to the trouble of tracking down my address to send me the note, he congratulated me for keeping my cool on *The Rosie O'Donnell Show*.

It wasn't only other finalists I heard from. Women I'd met through the Beef Cook-Off sent me congratulations, including the Kittitas County Cattlewomen, who jointly signed a card in which I was chided for not cooking with beef. "Happy Trails," wrote one. She and her daughter had been part of the Rodeo Grandmas on a television ad. Coincidentally, they had also been featured on *The Rosie O'Donnell Show*.

It seemed we bounced off each other's successes.

As for people putting the touch on me, only one person fell

into that category. She wrote, "Way to go! (now where's *my* share?)" That message was quickly softened by one that followed. A woman who had known my sister Emeline wrote, "Knowing a few of your sadnesses in life, I am glad to see some new and possibly fun experiences come your way."

I heard from writers, too. A man I'd met at a conference in Oregon, said, "I can't believe I know a celebrity!" Another wrote, "even vicarious fame has its rewards. Just KNOWING a million dollar winner has elevated me to an entirely new social status."

As for chicken jokes, the best one came hidden among a dozen long-stemmed red (plastic!) roses. In the middle of the arrangement was a full-scale rubber chicken. That "chicken" joined a braid of garlic and a chili pepper *ristra* to hang beside my pots and pans. It remained there until we moved. In fact, Loa remembers very little about that house except the rubber chicken.

My worries about whether dinner invitations would drop off now that I was a recognized cook were for naught. Our social life went into high gear. It seems that people wanted to hear my story. They also wanted to tell me theirs. Of how they heard, of who they had told, of whether they had seen me on television or heard me on a radio show.

Along with this I received chicken updates from across the country. Through the grapevine, I learned that I had been locked in a tie with Edwina Gadsby in the final stages of the judging process in Orlando. Some of the newspaper clippings that friends and strangers sent me went into the details. "Everyone who tasted it raved about Gadsby's cake, and judge chairman Susan Westmoreland of *Good Housekeeping* magazine later admitted that half of the judges favored the couscous chicken dish and the other half, the Brownie Soufflé Cake…they broke the tie by noting that the main dish entry 'was the better tasting and really does take 30 minutes' to get on the table."

This is not to say Edwina's recipe stretched the preparation time limit, but her white chocolate mint cream (which is delicious, by the way) has to chill for an hour before serving with her brownie soufflé.

Some reports told of the judges debating whether my recipe's African-inspired flavor would find acceptance among American cooks. They reported that Pillsbury had renamed my submission, changing it from Moroccan Chicken to Salsa Couscous Chicken to soften its impact. I don't know where this rumor came from. I wish I *had* named it Moroccan Chicken. Carolyn Jung, food editor of the *San Jose Mercury News*, would later write, "The judges argued back and forth for hours: Everyone loves dessert, couscous is too weird, cooks won't want to whip egg whites for the cake, cooks know that instant couscous is a no-brainer," and so forth. The last holdout, Sharon Dowell of the *Daily Oklahoman*, who initially preferred the dessert, finally cast the deciding vote for the chicken. "It was excruciating," she later wrote. "I cried after that one."

Poor Ms. Dowell. I hate to think I brought anyone to tears, but I have to admit I'm glad it went my way. At the same time, hearing about the judges' deliberation gave me a funny feeling of connection to Edwina. If the tie had been broken in her favor, I might never have been the wiser. I'd have taken home a check for $10,000, overjoyed and ready to fire up my stove for a try at the 2000 Bake-Off. Having won, though, I am now ineligible. As are Karen and Carl. Likewise, entrants are limited to three times as finalists, after which they—and their immediate families—become ineligible. For this reason, some people limit themselves to two tries as finalists, thus keeping their husbands or daughters or mothers in the running.

Scott Cherry of the *Tulsa World*, focused on why a main dish won over something sweet, quoting Susan Westmoreland. "Mathews' recipe was given a slight nod over the Fast & Easy Treats winner.... The two recipes were very clearly the finalists.... It came down to which one was better tasting and fit the quick and easy theme. The winner had a five-star taste." Several of the articles included the judges' praise for the complexity of my recipe's flavor with so few ingredients. Michael Booth wrote in the *Denver Post*, "One of the populist favorites...nearly bumped out Mathews for top honors. Judges said they debated well into the afternoon," while Heather McPherson of the *Orlando Sentinel* focused on my description of the process. "Finalists had from 9 a.m. to 2 p.m. to prepare their dishes. But most contestants were finished hours before their cooking stations were shut down. Befitting her cool demeanor, Mathews took her time. She made her Salsa Couscous Chicken three times—the first batch looked so good she sent it to be photographed; the second batch tasted good, so she sent it to the judges. But by the time she finished the third batch, which was for sampling by other finalists and onlookers, there were few people left to eat." Sounds like Goldilocks and the Three Bears.

My timing might explain the *Denver Post* calling my recipe "a bit of a sleeper." Hardly anyone had tried it.

Other reports focused on my reactions—or apparent lack thereof—at the winning moment. *The Oregonian* wrote, "Mathews didn't exactly jump for joy after winning." The *Norwich Bulletin* in Connecticut headlined me as the "frugal fiction writer" and pointed out, "she didn't blink an eyelash…Mathews showed no visible emotion when she heard her name…here's a woman whose feet are so firmly planted on the ground…I don't know about you, but I love Ellie Mathews." Cheramie Sonnier of *The Advocate* in Baton Rouge, Louisiana, wrote, "Cool and collected, Ellie Mathews only turned her head to the side and gave a demure smile.…" The *Seattle Times* even quoted Carl. "She's usually low-key about her cooking efforts. She'll say, 'This might not be very good.'"

Other clippings poured in, including a full page from a Spanish language paper, *La Opinión*. They headlined the story, "*Pollo en salsa gana millón de dólares*" with a subhead, "*Después de 18 años un plato principal gana premio mayor de la competencia de comida de Pillsbury.*" In the article I'm referred to as *la feliz ganadora*. The happy winner.

But the funniest clipping was from Seattle's alternative paper, the *Stranger*. In their week in review column, they wrote, "Rumors have already arisen among disgruntled runners-up that

Mathews plagiarized the recipe from Kurt Cobain." What the *Stranger*'s readers didn't know is that Kurt and Courtney had considered buying the house just north of Carl and me before they decided on the house where he would eventually end his life. So we were already connected. Or nearly so.

With so much mail pouring in, I failed to reply to everyone. But I did write the twelve contest judges. My lockup onstage had been eating away at me. I didn't want any of them to feel cheated that they had awarded the prize to someone who hadn't shown excitement. In the letter I copied to each of them, I wrote, "My husband videotaped the awards show...Wow! Did I ever appear paralyzed with disbelief. That wasn't *calm* the audience saw; it was *shock*....since then I've let out an occasional whoop of delight....I couldn't have had this experience without you."

REPORTS of chicken sightings kept coming in. My e-mail and phone lines buzzed. Excited to spill the details, people told me the how, why, and where of making the Recipe.

A friend called. "You'll never believe this," he said. "We were up on Orcas Island for the weekend, and we went to a friend's house for dinner. He served this really great chicken dish, so I said, 'This stuff is terrific. Where'd you get the recipe?'"

"Out of the paper," the host told him, "I'll show you," whereupon he produced the food section of the *Seattle Times*, and there was my photograph.

A poet friend from Idaho attended a potluck. This time it was the *Spokane Spokesman-Review* her friend flashed when the question arose. My friend said, "Wait a minute. I *know* that woman!"

An artist we know in Hawaii clipped the recipe without noticing who had originated it. She just thought it looked good. Later, when she was tipped off, she wrote me, "Ellie had a little pan / she poured in some couscous, a chicken thigh / and salsa too. Would this mix cook her goose? / She added this, a touch of that. A judge came up the aisle. / Was that a frown upon her face? / No—a million dollar smile!"

SALSA Couscous Chicken was being cooked up by the vatful. Fortunately no one served it to me. And I not to them. I had seen too much of the stuff too early in the morning for too many days in a row in high tension situations. On the plane home from Los Angeles, I had had the realization: if I served it to one I'd have to serve it to many. I decided then never to make it again unless Pillsbury asked for another demo.

That didn't cut down on my enthusiasm for others and their creativity with "my" recipe. Our vegetarian friends made it with tofu. Someone told me about making a halibut variation, which seemed especially fitting, since my original inspiration was a fish recipe. Another substituted quinoa for couscous. My sister Sylvia's hunting friend made it with pheasant, which I took to mean he was a cook willing to work with what he had at hand. And why not? That's what a recipe is for, as far as I'm concerned. A starting point.

Just as I no longer owned the news that I'd won the contest, I no longer controlled the recipe. Any good cook knows how to adapt. Pillsbury had already modified it. Toward the close of the Bake-Off, finalists had been given typed copies of their recipes to distribute. We'd been asked to use those copies to hand out rather than any copies of our own original pages, since Pillsbury's home economists had made slight refinements here and there among them. A few titles had been edited. Some contestants' instructional steps had been simplified, elaborated, or streamlined. Ingredient lists had been jiggled. For example, on mine, they suggested vegetable oil and raisins as possible substitutions for the olive oil and currants that I'd specified, and they instructed that the sautéed almonds should be removed from the skillet with a slotted spoon and set aside before browning the chicken. They also wanted my salsa and seasonings to be combined in a mixing bowl before being added to the skillet, where I'd glopped everything into the pan together. More than one Seattle cook reported to me that she'd forgotten the almonds altogether once they'd been set aside. Given their Quick and Easy theme, I felt Pillsbury had complicated the process unnecessarily. On the other hand, I'd signed a legal agreement that the company was the "sole owner of all my right and interest in the recipe."

It had been a fair exchange, and it was time for me to let go. And the best way to accomplish that was to think about the big, juicy prize the company had given me.

CHAPTER TWENTY-SEVEN

By kicking Carl and me into a higher tax bracket, fifty thousand a year figured out to be about a hundred dollars a day, a much easier figure for me to comprehend, an amount I began to remind myself of when contemplating everyday purchases—a shrub for the garden, a sweater, a book. But I couldn't possibly buy plants and books and sweaters every day. Nor did I want to.

We put ten thousand dollars each in accounts for Karen and Loa. The remaining money was poured into various existing joint accounts at home, keeping the IRS in mind and the well we hoped to have drilled at our cabin. With some of the remainder, I assumed we'd amp up the amounts we had been giving to various causes we support. There would be time to discuss all of this giving before the end of the tax year.

The cultural formulas of *win money; buy car*, and *win money; take trip* orbited around in my brain. New cars and luxury vacations are America's best solutions for disposing of wealth. But Carl and I had a car, a Toyota 4-Runner. We needed its beefy transmission to make it up the steep, rough road to our cabin. We were satisfied with our stripped-down answer to transportation and couldn't see replacing it for the sake of replacing it. As for the travel option, I'd had enough jetting around to last me a while, and I've never been attracted to cruises. All that water.

Before the contest, however, Carl and I had been intending to add a small pickup truck to our rolling stock. We'd been putting off the errand for a couple of months. The dust began to settle on my media whirl. Even the radio interview calls had diminished. So one Saturday in March, we headed out to Auto Row, checkbook in hand. We settled on a three-year-old Mazda, salsa red. My only splurge was in selecting a truck with a slightly more puffed-up interior than I might have otherwise chosen.

To balance that rather utilitarian purchase, we felt compelled to make a frivolous move. More than one friend was impatiently waiting for me to let loose, go on a spree, to show up wearing a new outfit or sporting a pair of dangly, gem-studded earrings. To do something silly. Outrageous, even.

The problem was that silly and outrageous isn't really me. My values were still my values. Winning the Bake-Off did not include a personality transplant. As I'd told the television reporter who pointed a microphone at me while standing in my pantry, I loved winning the Bake-Off because I'm fundamentally competitive, but I hoped the experience wasn't going to change me.

Carl and I both like fine china. One afternoon we headed downtown to a tableware store, almost dizzy with the idea of indulging ourselves in a set of new plates or a wild soup tureen or at least a few new mugs…or, or, or. Whatever struck our fancy. We could do that now. Never mind that we had a houseful of beautiful plates already. That wasn't the point. Money was burning a hole in our communal pocket.

We wandered around in that store more than an hour, looking and considering, considering and looking. Wedgwood. Royal Doulton. Lenox. Spode. Portmeirion. Gorgeous patterns. We could have scooped up whatever appealed. We held plates carefully in our hands, evaluated their translucence, examined their hallmarks, held them to window light.

Finally, Carl admitted, "We don't really need any of this, do we?"

"Yeah. It's feeling a bit forced."

"If we bought a bunch of china, we'd have to find a place to put the old stuff."

"I like the old stuff fine. Let's bail."

We left the store with a small, tin pail from Villeroy & Boch enameled with berries and cherries to coordinate with their French Garden pattern. We had no real use for it, but we both liked it. We bought it largely because we felt compelled to buy *some*thing. A couple of weeks later I began placing eggs in it to keep in the refrigerator, where it has been in service ever since. That ridiculous pail has taken on meaning, a reminder. Plus, it's a great solution to egg storage.

It may be too late for me, an old dog not elastic enough to learn new tricks. After nearly half a century of being clever with leftovers, remnants, and scraps, I'm stuck in thrift mode. That sort of training doesn't go away overnight.

Karen has a strategy for not buying what she doesn't need. She calls it catch-and-release shopping. I've adopted her method of placing an item in my cart, then walking around with it in my possession while looking at other merchandise. I think about buying it. I imagine myself buying it. When it comes time to check out, however, I realize it's not for me and I replace it on the shelf or rack from which it came. This leaves me with the fun of having had the fantasy of taking something new home, without the hassle of finding a place to put it once I get there.

Don't get me wrong. I love having the money. I love the security it gives me, the options. I loved being able to forgive the loan we'd made to Karen when she bought her house. I love being able to consider a sixteen-thousand-dollar trip to the Antarctic, even if we decide not to take it. I love that Carl doesn't have to work anymore if he doesn't want to. But he does want to work, because he finds his work satisfying, and I love him for that.

My luxuries come more in the form of a hole in the ground. In April, after the snow had cleared on the road leading to our cabin, we arranged for the local well driller to pay a call.

People have different methods of selling their services. Some create an atmosphere of solving problems; others focus on problems you didn't know were there.

"Ah-h-yupp," the well driller said, surveying our hill, "I'm going to need to get my truck up here."

"No problem," we said. "We can unlock the gate across the road anytime."

"Ah-h-yupp," he said, "I'm a-gonna need to figure out where to drill."

"No problem," we said. "We'll go with your recommendation." We tried to indicate a rough sense of how our forty acres lay. We tried to convey how flexible we could be.

"Wee-e-l-ll," he said. "It'll cost you."

"No problem," we said. "We have the money. Whatever it takes."

"You know," he said, 'you're gonna need a pump to bring the water out of the ground."

At about this point, I began to wonder how this guy stayed in business. Of course we would need a pump. Who doesn't need a pump to bring up water from a well? What did he take us for? But Carl's and my imaginations were dazzled with the image of our cup runneth over. The idea of clear, drinkable water gushing from the ground—or even dribbling enough to accumulate—had us salivating. We had struggled with a Mickey Mouse setup for ten years. With a gas-powered rig, we'd been pumping river water up our hill in two noisy, time-consuming stages to achieve a gravity-fed system using a stock tank. Never mind the time a squirrel had drowned and decomposed in the tank during our absence one spring. All those little bones.

The well driller rubbed the back of his neck and studied the horizon. "You know," he said, "these things are never easy."

The more this guy cluttered up our ponderosa atmosphere, the more I began to value the crummy water setup that had been serving us all along. After all, scrambling up and down our hill kept Carl and me in good shape. The uncertainty of whether the system would fail gave us a sense of accomplishment each time it didn't. Who needs a well? There are people the world over who live without running water. I couldn't wait to get that man and his negative energy out of my realm.

Unfortunately, there were only two drillers in the area, and the other one never returned our calls. A couple of years after that we would decide to sell the property. For the period of time when we'd been involved in building the place, the process had practically defined us. Now, with the cabin and the road to it complete, it was all about maintenance: keeping the roof clear of snow in winter and the rinky-dink water system running in summer. Combine that with the fear of forest fire, the occasional rattlesnake sighting, bears tearing our window screens, and general upkeep, and the retreat that was meant to be all about relaxing was beginning to feel burdensome.

The intrigue of nonelectric living would lose its luster, too. I was devoting more and more time to writing, and that necessitated access to a computer. Even with a laptop running on batteries, crafting manuscripts by kerosene lamplight wasn't for me.

Right around the time of the goat rodeo with the well man came the news that the Seattle Arts Commission had awarded my essay "Counting to Forty-Seven" its largest honor: $7,500 and an opportunity for a public reading.

It's not unusual for writers to submit samples of their work to competitions. I had submitted my essay to this one months before. The notice came in the form of a letter. Our mail was usually delivered midafternoon. I could see the carrier's truck from my desk. I opened the envelope on my way back into the house, expecting a routine thanks-but-no-thanks form letter. Then I'd turn my attention to the catalogs or bills or whatever else was in my hand. Instead, I read just the opposite. I'd won. My essay was about being with my mother the day she died.

If Pillsbury wanted proof that I'm capable of shrieking and screaming, they needed only to have been within a block or so of my house that day. Carl, who had been working in his office on the third floor when I brought in the mail, took the stairs down to the main floor two at a time, fearing I'd been injured. The vocalization of my spontaneous combustion was that dramatic.

As it happened, some of the money from that award found its way out of my account and into that of a literary journal that scrapes by on donations. One that would eventually reject my work a dozen or more times.

Chapter Twenty-eight

I can't say whether it was the *magna cum laude* cooking prize I'd won or the attention that followed, but I became cocky. I thought I had the knack, the touch, the inside track, and since Pillsbury wasn't the only game in town, I turned to see who else I could play with.

Not too long after the Bake-Off, Progresso Soup announced its Great Discovery contest. The grand prize was $20,000 for a new flavor that the company promised to put into production. Well, I thought. Coming up with that should be a snap. My only hesitation was whether it would be fair to win another big prize so soon.

I didn't hesitate for long. I dusted off my stockpot, laid in a supply of onions, beans, barley, bacon, beef bones, and chicken backs—all the good old-fashioned elements of a nice potage—

rolled up my sleeves, turned on my back burner, and put my brain into high gear while trying to imagine what could be done in the name of soup that hadn't been done before.

The distinction between a cook-off and a recipe contest is that the former is one in which finalists assemble somewhere to prepare their entries to be judged, while the latter is simply a mail-in arrangement judged without the contestant's further participation. This one wouldn't even require that I travel. It wasn't a cook-off. (Pillsbury retains exclusive use of the term *Bake-Off*.)

Keeping in mind what I thought would gracefully survive the canning process, I developed six recipes. Roasted Lemon Chicken Soup was wonderfully deep in flavor with dark-meat chicken and caramelized onion and plenty of potato with herbs and, of course, the lemon promised in the title. Then there was a Red Lentil Soup—vegetarian! This was built on an East Indian theme as opposed to what Progresso was already doing with lentils in the Italian direction. But because Progresso has Italian leanings, I threw together a version of Puttanesca Soup, robust in its beefiness and with plenty of garlic and red pepper flakes and kalamata olives and anchovy paste and capers. Sticking with the international mindset, just in case the sponsor wanted something truly out there, I submitted African Groundnut, with peanuts and yam and tomato sweetened with apple juice. If they preferred to reach back a generation, I gave them Grandmother's Lima Bean Soup, which I thought was darned good. My favorite of all, however, and what I thought had the best chance, was Wintergarden Soup. I was in love with the name, the flavor, the old-fashioned vegetables I'd dared to put in it: leeks, turnips, parsnips, cauliflower, horseradish—all enriched with a cream base. It was a sure winner.

Instead, the judges chose a recipe called Southwestern Style Corn Chowder. I didn't make second place or third place, or any place. Not even honorable mention. I was back to square one, and I'm convinced it was ultimately good for me to be brought down a peg.

But some do have the knack. The Gadsbys' names, for example, turn up over and over on winners lists. Others' names show up with astonishing regularity. The Gadsbys are not the only husband and wife team, sometimes competing with each other. Sister and sister, mother and daughter, mother and son—entire dynasties can be tracked from National Beef to National Chicken to Catfish to Garlic to Burgers to Rice. The same surnames show up over and over in contests across the nation.

This leads to a network of sorts. Cook-off finalists meet and stay in touch, meet again, compete again, cheer each other on. As with any interest, clubs, newsletters, and Internet sites keep the gossip channels lit up. It's a refreshingly friendly and supportive community.

For a while I thought I'd plunge in full force. I like to cook. I like to compete. After the Progresso failure, I caught sight of a couple more contests, had some ideas, worked them up in the kitchen, but never got to the point of submitting. For me the hard part is getting the recipe written up and formatted in accordance with the rules. One sponsor might want your name and address on the recipe, another on a separate card of specific dimensions. One wants ingredients listed in order of use, another wants its product listed first. Some require proof of purchase. Some restrict the number of entries, number of servings, number of ingredients. The fine print is not to be taken lightly. This is where I get bogged down.

Also, there's my ever-present fear of grease. Many contest judges are from the restaurant world, where indulgence is the norm. I remember hearing a radio interview with a hotshot chef. While demonstrating a soup recipe (by radio!), he put in a shocking amount of butter. The interviewer questioned this.

"Oh, but it tastes so good," the chef said. "And besides, your guests will never know."

I call this cooking without a conscience. When you think about it, it's an act of faith to eat something prepared by a stranger. We trust each other to wash the lettuce, sift out the rodent hairs, and generally keep the well-being of a human body in mind.

Contest judges don't always factor in cost, practicality, and wholesomeness. I look at some winning recipes and wince. Load anything up with enough fat and sugar and it'll be delicious. But.

Some contests get around the calorie count on a technicality: they cut the servings microscopically small before publicizing the nutritional breakdown. An eight-inch pie, for example, might show four hundred or so calories per serving. That doesn't seem out of line until you look at the number of servings they've microtomed that little puppy into. A sixteenth of an eight-inch pie is likely to look pretty lost once it hits the plate. How you'll convince your guests that it's not a sample of more to come will be up to you. Bury that buttery pastry dough in sugar, sour cream, chocolate chips, walnuts, and caramel topping, and—sure—it'll taste great. But.

Do the math. Bake a batch of brownies in a nine-by-thirteen-inch pan and cut the results into thirty-six pieces. Call each a serving. Never mind that it'll be less than half the size of your heart surgeon's business card. Then look at the nutritional breakdown. For caloric wallop it'll compare more to a Snickers bar or a Butterfinger than anything that used to come out of Grandma's oven in the name of cakes and cookies. The lesson is this: just because you *can* add cream cheese and peanut butter to everything, whether savory or sweet, doesn't mean you ought to.

This is not to say that some contests don't focus on health and good eating. And bless those that do. Each sponsor creates its own unique culture. Some want convenience while others want *haute cuisine*. One will emphasize an all-American, Mom and apple pie slant while others reward contestants for pairing chicken with watermelon and feta cheese. Some contests are judged by professional chefs while others are judged by the sponsors themselves, whether they are in the processed cheese business or instant pudding or frozen fish.

They all follow trends. It's about discovery. It's about newness. It's about invention. A while ago the smoky flavor of chipotle chilies showed up in everything except toothpaste and soda pop. Before that it was balsamic vinegar. Chai is big these days, as is anything made with green tea. Wasabi, which isn't even real wasabi in most cases but green-colored horseradish, has been making it big, too. It seems we possess a never-ending fascination with new sensations. Who can say what's about to come over the crest of the next hill?

The question is, who can spot it first?

We're a nation of challengers, constantly measuring ourselves against each other to determine who's the biggest/fastest/smartest/prettiest beer drinker, movie editor, ski jumper, aria singer, hockey player, sonnet writer, arm wrestler, crossword puzzler, or teenage drama queen. Whether participating or kibitzing from the sidelines, competition seems to be in our blood. So, when KING-TV's *Evening Magazine* came along, asking me to participate in a show all about contest winners, I agreed.

Evening Magazine is hosted by a couple of affable clowns. These men ferret out oddballs and moments of entertaining interest around the Northwest and add them up to thirty minutes of airtime, Monday through Friday.

I did not relish the idea of getting cozy with another pot of Salsa Couscous Chicken, but that was part of the formula. A crew from the station arrived at my house. We did a little Q&A while the tape rolled, and I brandished a wooden spoon while standing at my stove, then invited the show's host to sit down at my china and crystal setup for a sample. He tucked in his napkin, took his obligatory bite, and looked directly at the camera with a smirk. "Hmmm," he said. "Tastes a little like chicken." Then he calmly proceeded to eat all that I'd served him. Nothing but bones on the plate by the time he and his crew had packed up and gone.

His lunch that day was more than show business. The camera's red light had clicked off after the first bite.

Chapter Twenty-nine

There must have been something in the air. Oprah's crew had the same idea as *Evening Magazine*. They, too, wanted a show about contest winners.

Fifty-one weeks after winning the Bake-Off, I agreed to fly to Chicago on two days' notice.

I didn't know what to expect. At first it seemed as if I'd be involved in another dump and stir for the cameras. Then the format shifted. Maybe I'd be sitting on the couch with Oprah, therapist style. Then it shifted again. Then I decided simply to present my body to the situation and let things sort themselves out on the fly. And they did fly.

Besides the Bake-Off, *Evening Magazine* had focused on contests with prizes on the level of a stereo, a pair of binoculars, a big-screen television, a dishwasher, a motorcycle, a weekend trip to the coast. There was a raffle for a house, and a trip for two to Germany to see the Rolling Stones, but most of the contests featured on that show were penny ante compared to the Bake-Off. Some were out-and-out gross. A Seattle radio host had held a competition called How Far Will You Go? Whoever was deemed to have committed the most outrageous act won a car. One couple submitted a video of themselves playing naked Twister. Another cleaned their Chevy Blazer with their tongues. A family of four shaved their heads, covered their scalps in molasses, and invited cows to lick them clean. But the man who won was a high school principal from Oregon who allowed himself to essentially take a bath in fresh Tillamook County cow manure. Yuck.

I was flown to Chicago, whisked to the Omni Hotel in a white limousine, given a fifty-dollar chit for dinner at the hotel and one half that size for breakfast. My room was a lavish arrangement of marble and satiny finishes: a separate parlor, two televisions, library shelves with real books, a complete wet bar, and a bed the size of Rhode Island.

I had never before ordered from room service. Fifty dollars for dinner seemed a staggering amount. I was convinced I wouldn't make a dent. I ordered modestly from the bottom of the menu, but by the time the service fee was added, and the automatic gratuity, the taxes, and the expected tip on top of it all, I hit the high forties, and that was without wine. Lesson learned.

I think a lot about food, especially when I'm traveling. Then, more than ever, if I don't eat well, I won't feel well. A tummy ache is hardly the end of the world, but in a hotel and when I'm about to meet a bunch of new people? No thanks.

Everyone has his own idea of what constitutes a good meal. For some the pleasure is in the sauces; others might focus mainly on the flesh portion of the menu. For me, the measure of a meal is all in the vegetables, possibly to an obsessive level. Sometimes, when at the mercy of a commercial kitchen's offerings, I have the fantasy of finding a mountain of perfectly steamed carrots or asparagus nestled against a single boiled potato. Imagine a chef who describes not only what waters his fish once swam in or what his lambs once grazed on, but whether his broccoli was open-pollinated, Calabrese or Green Goliath.

I settled on "Salmon in Lime-Ginger *Beurre Blanc*." Room Service arrived with a hunk of fish big enough to top up my Omega-3s into the next decade. That serving of salmon took command of the plate, swimming as it did in its own private lake of yellow sauce, and members of the plant kingdom had been relegated to decoration: a couple of zucchini slivers, three translucent carrot embryos, a spatter of parsley around the rim. As for the truth-in-advertising reality check, there was no hint of lime or ginger or *beurre* to be found in the flavors of that meal.

With their foofs and poofs of garnishes, the hotel seemed bent on providing me a dining experience, when all I wanted was a solution to hunger. Too often, when on the road, whether ordering upscale or down-home, it seems impossible to find what Carl and I call clean food, food that isn't oversauced, oversweetened, or overdressed. But then, as I've admitted, I'm the person who goes for the boiled stuff when under stress. And I don't mind saying I felt a bit edgy about coming face-to-face with Oprah. She's a force, an American icon.

Not that I don't sauce and season when cooking in my own kitchen. Witness the very recipe I'd been flown to Chicago to talk about. But there are ways and there are ways. If it is an act of faith to eat food prepared by someone whose eyes you've never met, it's faith raised to another power when calling down from the tenth floor.

I had just tucked into my salmon when Oprah's producer rang my room to discuss what I should expect in the morning.

"A limousine will pick you up and take you to the studio. You should arrive with your face and hair washed but without any makeup," she said. She went on to explain that Oprah and company were just back from a junket to the Bahamas so they were a little discombobulated. "Tomorrow's show is going to be all contest winners," she said. "So we'll put you in with the audience and Oprah will call on you one by one. Okay?"

"Fine," I said. I had nothing at stake in how they made their program. I was primarily there for Pillsbury's benefit. I'd also arranged to meet an editor for lunch after I'd done my part for furthering Old El Paso Salsa.

"There's one question I don't want to be asked," I told the producer. I'd become a little savvier since my first experiences on television.

"And what might that be?"

"I would like it if no one asked me what I did with the money."

"You're the one with the million?" I could hear her flipping through papers. "The Pillsbury woman? I'll make a note of it."

IN the morning a mother, father, and seven-year-old girl who had won fifty grand in a giggle contest piled into the limousine with me. They were clearly caught up in the trappings of the moment, marveling over the white leather seats, the ooh-la-la of it all. I, on the other hand, was suffering from early-morning jet lag, and I felt very much aware of being someone's piece of promotional property.

Harpo (*Oprah* spelled backward) Studios is a renovated armory and looks every bit the part, a low, sturdy-looking building with the name of the show on the awning. We were ushered through the lobby where eager audience members would later line up, and into a dressing and makeup area where an assembly line was in progress.

When my turn came up, no one asked how I usually groom myself. Pffft went the hairspray. On went the lipstick, the rouge, the colored eye shadow. Oh, well, I thought, this isn't about the real me anyway. I thought it best to go with the flow, and I could hardly blame them for rushing us through; there were a lot of us slated to appear on the show.

Getting combed by its owner was a black and white pooch that had taken first place at the Westminster Dog Show. That dog fit in its own silver trophy—not that the dog was small, but the trophy was large, as was the Best in Show purple ribbon rosette. Triplet two-year-old girls, as done up as that dog, looked as if they might want to play with the dog, but it didn't seem to be that kind of pet.

There were other children as well. When the rest of us were assigned to audience seats for the start of the show, child winners and their parents stayed offstage to be called in as their turns unfolded.

As with the awards show at the Bake-Off, we were assigned to seats in accordance with the floor director's chart of who was who, so that when our turns came up the camera could locate the right face. Not that I would have been confused with the man who had won a Garth Brooks look-alike contest.

By having us sit with regular audience members, we were swept up in their frenzy for seeing the star of the show. I'd entered a temple of America's popular culture. The congregants were buzzing.

The warm-up man came onstage ahead of Oprah's appearance. "When she comes in," he said, "I want this section here to stand." He pointed to the side where I sat. "And then this section." He pointed to the middle seats. "And then this section." He pointed to the other side. "It'll be like a wave."

When I went to the Bake-Off I'd gone as an observer. Here, too, I'd have preferred to keep to the shadows while watching the parade go by. Now I'd become part of the parade. When I signed up to do that gig I didn't know I'd be expected to stand up and cheer, but stand up and cheer I did. And the other hundred or so in the studio were fervently following along with what the warm-up man wanted. We were not mere observers. Our responses were an integral part of the show. Emotion on cue.

Oprah opened with a tribute to Gene Siskel, a fellow Chicagoan who had died that weekend. Then, to kick off the contest theme, she showed off the 7.2-carat diamond ring she was sporting. For the briefest moment, she let her fans think she might be on the verge of announcing an engagement, then she explained the ring was actually to be given away by Godiva Chocolatier via Willy Wonka's golden ticket method. That stone was a hunky, chunky item, setting off sparkles all over the studio. Someone somewhere out there in consumerland would buy the box of sweets into which the coupon for the ring had been slipped, and the ring would be theirs. Oprah flashed the bauble this way and that, admiring the fireworks.

It was already time for the first commercial break, and here's where I noticed a big difference between this and my experiences with the *Rosie* show and *Crook & Chase*. On those I was ushered in and out for my segment only. Standing with those hosts, I had faced the audience. Here, I was the audience. I saw all the mechanics of making the show. A veritable army of technicians and directors moved silently around the studio orchestrating the proceedings with hand gestures and wireless communications.

When the red light on the main camera went off, a handful of assistants descended on Oprah. One applied powder to her face, another handed her pages of script, still another straightened her dress. Her demeanor changed, too. All business. Her focus was off the audience. The high energy and bright smile we're used to seeing from our living rooms was given over to a look of concentration.

Two and a half minutes later she was back. The giggle-off girl who had been in the limousine with me bounced onto the set to do her number. Next an opera singer with a howling poodle appeared on a huge screen for a video remote interview. Many of the featured contests came with their own promotional video clips, like the $50,000 wedding/honeymoon package given away by *Brides* magazine.

French's, the mustard company, had sponsored a Make a Funny Face contest, offering a trip for two to Napa Valley. The winner had constructed an elaborate arrangement of foodstuffs to form a face, using pigs in blankets as curly hair. *America's Funniest Home Video*, which netted someone a $100,000 check, featured a child who cried every time his father sang (which begs the question, why would the father continue to sing?) and a setup of people walking into plate glass they didn't think was there. Dr. Scholl's had run a competition for Best-Looking Feet. The winner removed a high-heeled sandal and Oprah stroked the woman's arch. More singing kids, who had vied for Oscar Mayer's $20,000. A group of rappers won Lever Brothers' five grand for singing in the shower. On the subject of wrapping, Scotch brand tape had awarded $10,000 for the best and fastest and most creative gift wrap. Only in America!

Then came Kirby the Papillon of Westminster Dog Show fame, followed by the winner of Kellogg's Crunch-a-thon, a man who had executed 6,125 abdominal crunches in Times Square over a period of three hours. He willingly lifted his shirt so Oprah could get some hands-on time with his abs. America's Funniest Mom made faces for $10,000. Then came the pink-and-lace-dressed triplets who had been judged most alike at Ohio's Twin Festival, followed by a pair of adult twins, also winners of most alike. The Garth Brooks and Reba McEntire look-alikes claimed some connection to Oprah's father's barbershop.

I had no idea when to expect my turn. Oprah had a microphone that didn't pick up background noise, which allowed her to talk audibly to the viewing audience during periods of applause, when she wasn't audible to us in the studio. Not hearing her introductions, it was hard to anticipate when to take a preparatory breath.

When my bit finally came, she began with a video clip of people chopping and stirring at the Bake-Off while she read an explanation of the contest's structure. Then bam! she found me in the audience. I was on.

Right up front she asked, "Whadja do with the money?"

So much for my one request. If we had been talking as equals, I might have lobbed back a good natured reminder, but this was television's version of conversation. And I was the guest; she was my host.

"I spent some, I saved some, I gave some away," I said. A Teflon reply and one she wasn't prepared for, but we recovered into some easy chitchat. I didn't mean to throw her off guard. I think she had a tough show to run that day with umpteen guests, a dog, and a funeral to attend in the afternoon.

Just then a phalanx of tuxedo-dressed servers emerged from the Harpo Studios wings while balancing trays of paper sample cups. I couldn't see what they were bearing, but my focus was on responding to Oprah. She asked, "What did you bake?" Of course, I hadn't baked a thing, but it's a natural question, given the contest's name. While I tried to explain that the Bake-Off isn't only about baking, the servers began circulating through the audience. When I'd passed from the greenroom to the set earlier, I'd noticed, out of the corner of my eye, some stainless steel caterers trays steaming in the lobby. I didn't know that Oprah's very own personal chef had prepared my stovetop dish. Apparently her staff hadn't briefed the star of the show either; she was as surprised as I was. If a picture speaks a thousand words, a sample speaks a million. Funny that I hadn't recognized Salsa Couscous Chicken when I'd walked past it in the lobby. It has a very distinctive aroma.

A day or two later, after I'd flown home, I called Marlene Johnson to apologize. I felt I might have let Pillsbury down by not striking the right chord with Oprah, by not being more fun in front of the camera.

"Don't worry," she said. "What matters to us is that Oprah took a bite of the dish on national television and said that it tasted delicious."

Chapter Thirty

With my *Oprah* appearance coming a year after the Bake-Off, surely it would be my last act as the reigning queen of chickendom. Then food writer Amanda Hesser called. She was planning an article for the *New York Times Magazine*. She wanted to examine whether cooking contest winners were trend-setters or trend followers, asking when, for example, everyone had gone nuts with green, red, and yellow bell peppers in everything. Before or after they showed up at the Bake-Off?

As plans progressed, the concept for the article morphed from fashion *in* food to fashion *and* food. A photographer was going to come to my house to take my picture. Phone calls back and forth had me answering more questions about my dress and shoe sizes than the size of my kitchen. That seemed weird.

Wouldn't I wear my own clothes for the pictures? Maybe they were offering to doll me up, do a makeover as a way to put me at ease. I figured once the photographer arrived and saw that I was presentable all on my own, the details would iron themselves out. Things like that usually do. If history were a guide, the interest would be more in my chicken dish than in me anyway.

When you get right down to it, there's not a lot to say about a chicken dish, and once you've snuggled a camera up to it for a shot or two, there's not a lot more to show. Oprah had proved this when she took her staged bite. The production of her show is clearly the result of incredible teamwork. Her staff points her in a direction and she takes off. Only occasionally during that show did she seem to ad-lib. When she sampled the salsa chicken, however, she might have been running off track. To be fair, her specialty is the human side of things, guests who come to her couch to teach us how to lead a better life. Oprah knows what to do with them. But a Bake-Off cook? What's to talk about? Oprah responded to her bite of chicken by repeating, "very good," and, "really very good," and, "very, very good." This was interspersed with "a million dollars" said with different intonations of incredulity all twelve times.

I was certain the *New York Times* would represent the opposite end of the media spectrum, with a willingness to delve into the nuances of cinnamon and cumin while leaving the human drama of winning big money to speak for itself.

It took a slew of phone calls to get a plan nailed down. First, Ms. Hesser interviewed me, and that was exciting because she knew how to talk about food. Next, Martha Camarillo, the photographer, started calling. She would be sweeping the nation in one gulp, stopping in half a dozen states to catch the other winners targeted for the article, so it took a while for her to coordinate her itinerary with everyone. Each time she called, Martha verified my clothing and shoe sizes.

"What gives?" I said to the young man renting our spare room at the time. He was the son of an old friend who had emigrated to Australia before she began her family. Rob was only twenty-two, but he had been all over the world. He was a foodie's foodie; maybe due to the Aussie influence, where I think some of the biggest leaps have been happening in world cuisine. Rob was also pretty media savvy.

"I'm not wearing somebody else's clothes," I said to him in anticipation of Martha's arrival.

"No," he said. "I wouldn't think so. Don't knuckle under to that East Coast crowd."

I'd made the declaration more to myself than to him, but by having said it out loud, it almost became a pact.

Martha called the night before our appointment. She'd arrived in Seattle with her assistant and Avena Gallagher, a stylist.

"A stylist?" I said.

"She'll dress you."

I hung up and dug in my heels even deeper on the clothing issue. What I didn't know was that these guys were big-time hotshots. On the subject of what to wear, they were ready to trump just about any little ace I thought I had up my sleeve.

They arrived in the morning with three duffel bags, practically the size of my dining room table and stuffed as full as sausages. Martha had a Hasselblad and all that went with it: lights, tripods, power cords, boxes of film, cases of lenses. There's more to taking a picture than pressing the shutter. All this for me?

In a matter of minutes those three women had overtaken most of my house.

"We'll do our first setup in here," said Martha, indicating the dining room. She said it to Avena, not to me. I was a bit player in that scene.

Avena had already burst open her bags of fashion, borrowed from some clearinghouse in New York City. Christian Dior, Tommy Hilfiger, Jean Paul Gautier. These weren't copies, either; they were the real thing. All the magazine had to do was agree to give full credit to the designers in exchange for borrowing whatever fashion they wanted. Those bags were crammed with thousands and thousands of dollars' worth of garments.

Avena already had the assistant steaming wrinkles out of clothes in Carl's and my bedroom. "How about this on her?" she asked Martha, holding up a garment. I'd hesitate to call it a blouse, but at the very least it was intended to be worn on the upper part of the body, gold lamé with embroidered linen handkerchief insets. The handkerchiefs were torn along one edge.

I panicked. Karen had come to watch the goings-on. She is a natural-born peacemaker, the mediator of all mediators. "My mother's most comfortable in jeans," she warned, hoping my natural-born rebellious streak wouldn't surface.

I stood at the doorway to my bedroom. Oddball getups were

draped over the doors to our two closets, our bathroom, our bed. "Should I go ahead and make the chicken?" I asked, hoping to divert attention from the clothes.

Sure, sure, they answered. That would be fine. But they were not to be diverted by anything as humdrum as kitchen work.

I don't think it ever dawned on those three New York dynamos that I wasn't inclined to leap into their outrageous clothes. It never dawned on me that I would.

Downstairs, I relaxed by stirring up a batch of chicken. At least I knew how to do that. I set the dining table with my blue china. I put on the dog, layering tablecloth upon tablecloth, polishing the silver, setting out the cut crystal, fitting fresh candles into my Orrefors holders. I brought out a wine bottle to add to the staging, sliced bread for a basket, created the illusion of salad by arranging lettuce leaves in a bowl—all for the sake of the picture.

None of that made much of a dent in the buzz upstairs. Avena held clothes up to me, evaluating. Forget that chicken stuff. "We'll get a shot of that later," she said.

It was all about fashion. Little by little, for the sake of getting along, I yielded, agreeing to try this and then that. Clothes with big polka dots painted on, feathers sticking out, hand-painted scenes, oversized sequins. "What kind of shoes do you have?" they asked. Like a five-year-old set loose in her mother's closet, it was as if the big kids had asked me to play dress-up with them.

Rob came home. He watched in amused silence as I posed in

an outrageous costume, then he pulled me aside. "So much for integrity, ay?" he said with an easy smile.

Okay, so I was a sellout. My first real boss had taught me you have to choose your battles. I'd relaxed. The minute I shoved my ego out of the way I found I could join in the fun. As Carl would have said, you can't *buy* an experience like that. Unless a Dior original showed up at the Goodwill, it would be the closest I'd ever come to wearing one.

The photo session ended up taking all day. It took me half of that day to realize this wasn't going to be about chicken or Pillsbury or even food, except in the most nominal way. It wasn't even about me. This was high-concept silliness. This was art. This was New York comes to Ellie's house.

It was Martha's first contract with the *New York Times Magazine*, and she wanted the results to solidify her new relationship with them. My usual way of dressing myself, my little chicken recipe, my big-deal prize were not the main event. What she wanted was the shot. She was in charge of how the article would look, and she had something specific in mind.

I don't think I got it until the quilted oven mitts came out. Avena had them in lavender, magenta, and aqua. "Here," she said. "Put these on." She handed me the pink pair.

I was wearing a Jean Paul Gautier jersey wrap dress, available at Saks Fifth Avenue for $985, a length of Martin Margiela pearls that reached my waist, and a fabric "brooch" by At Four. It looked like a cross between Kirby's Best in Show rosette and a nylon net pot scrubber. Clearly, by adding the oven mitts, this crew had a kind of avant-garde exaggeration in mind.

Oh. This was meant to be over the top. Tongue-in-cheek was an attitude I could get behind. Bring back the shredded lamé.

We did about three setups, the last of which had me in a pullover vest made of wool jersey and ostrich feathers. Some of us thought they should have been chicken feathers to go with my dish. As for the dish of chicken I'd prepared? Eventually, Martha got around to that requisite shot. No one was interested in tasting it, though.

The article didn't come out for quite a while after that. Only then was I able to see how Martha and Avena had styled the other Bake-Off participants featured in the story. All of us were looking straight-on to the camera in an otherworldly sort of way. And all of us were wearing ridiculous clothes.

What a relief to realize that article wasn't about me and how I actually look or dress. *Oprah* wasn't about me or my chicken either. It was about Oprah. And *Rosie* was about Rosie. The media needs material to fill its space and time slots. They need to borrow the rest of us and put us on their daily plates. Borrow our names, our accomplishments, our fifteen minutes of fame. We can choose to go along for the ride or not.

This was especially evident when I saw myself in the pages of the *New York Times Magazine* when it came out. My picture had been printed backward, me in the big pink mitts, me standing in my done-up dining room looking out at the world in mirror image. Something about layout, probably, about how the photograph fit the page in relation to the binding.

There are cultures in the world where people believe a camera steals a person's soul. What would they think it would do to them to be flipped over like that?

I didn't care, though. The picture was a hoot. That day had been a hoot. I had been involved in professional photo shoots before, but never one like that. Martha and Avena were fabulous to work with. A little wild, a little outrageous, maybe even a tiny bit manipulative—but in the nicest possible way. They had to be. It was their job.

A few weeks after appearing on the Oprah show, I received a letter. "Thank you for being a guest on the show," it said. "We appreciate your taking time to share yourself with our viewers and studio audience." At the bottom was Oprah's four-inch signature.

I imagined a giant stack of form letters with Oprah hurriedly scrawling her big, wild O in the signature space across each. The letter was a nice gesture, but I wondered: by the time she touched her fat-tipped pen to the bottom of that page did she remember me, or what I might have shared with her viewers and studio audience?.

With Oprah's high-tension life being what it is, of course, it's hard to know. It's possible she hadn't known who I was the day I'd been there. But that's okay. I know who I am. I'm the same person as before any of this happened.

Richer for the experience, though.

EPILOGUE

When the second of my $50,000 payments was due, Pillsbury offered me a choice. They could either buy an annuity in my name or cash me out for the cost of the annuity, which would have been $581,497. Counting the $50,000 I'd received the day of the awards show, the cash-out option would have put a total of $631,497 in my pocket by the end of the first year. I could spend the money or invest it on my own.

I went for the annuity. Having that choice gave me one more reason to respect the company and how they operate. I'm convinced there are no slippery moves, no tricks up their sleeve. Pillsbury puts on the contest fair and square, honors its word throughout, and treats its former Bake-Off participants with tremendous consideration and thoughtfulness.

No one carries it off on the same scale as Pillsbury, but my (limited) experience with other contests has been the same. On the up-and-up. No shenanigans. Not that I've entered all that many. In 2001 the company that makes Dreyer's ice cream (which uses the name Edy's in the eastern half of the country) announced a search for new flavor ideas. They wanted a name, a description, and fifty words characterizing Grandma's kitchen—presumably in reference to ice cream. I sent six submissions, and my Berry Patch Spice was selected as one of the ten finalists vying for $10,000. My concept was berry cobbler à la mode: pastry bits and blackberry puree swirled in a cinnamon ice cream base. My actual grandmother was a feminist and author, but not an enthusiastic cook. So I conjured up a gingham-curtain image of summer and sweets and someone else's ancestry for my fifty words.

Dreyer's flew Carl and me to Houston for a lavish weekend that included something of an ice cream–off, assisted greatly by the company's technical staff. Among the nine other finalists was Edwina Gadsby. I'm sure she knew as well as I that the two of us had been tied for Pillsbury's grand prize. The prospect of coming face-to-face with her felt exceedingly nervous-making. I feared she might resent me.

But she is a bigger-hearted person than that, it turns out. She and her husband were delightful company, fun to pal around with as the ice cream weekend progressed. Others, too, were upbeat and appealing. If I had reason to seek a whole new community of friends, I know exactly where I'd start. There's something about the fearlessness of creativity that makes a person interesting.

People assume I'm entering contests left and right. But I'm not. After Dreyer's I tried a couple more—nothing major—but didn't place. Coming up with ideas and recipes is fun, but it's work, too. Sometimes I get going on a concept, then fizzle out. Laziness, maybe.

One of the competitions I tried for was Sutter Home Winery's Build a Better Burger. The company has held the contest each September since 1990. James McNair, cookbook author extraordinaire, has been the head judge since the beginning and, unlike the "fast and quick" theme of many contests, he takes a no-holds-barred approach to ingredients and methods. Year after year, the recipes selected are elaborate, with ingredients lists that stretch from here to Kansas and back.

McNair has published over thirty books, some of which I've been using, recommending, and giving as gifts for years. I wanted to meet this man. In 2005 my take on Vietnamese sandwiches, which I called Grilled Pork Burgers Indochine, was selected as one of five nonbeef burgers for the cook-off. Sutter Home flew Carl and me to the Napa Valley for another lavish weekend. And I mean lavish. The Gadsbys weren't there, although both Bob and Edwina had been participants in earlier years. Norita Solt was there, though. She had been a finalist with me at the Bake-Off in Orlando. And the Food Network was there. In full force. They had six camera crews. Win or lose, I was destined to appear on national television once again.

As with the Bake-Off, my goal was to become a finalist, to go to the party. I wanted to meet James McNair. I had no intention of winning. I am not a barbecuer. The only grill I own is a beat-up Smokey Joe. I developed my recipe in a frying pan, figuring if I were selected as a finalist I'd get it together to learn how to cook over charcoal.

When the five of us lined up onstage for the award presentation, I stood immediately to McNair's right. He would be reading the winner's name from a card he held. During his introductory remarks, he was looking straight at me, which I took to mean he didn't want to be looking at the winner. Nevertheless, I determined that if he *did* say my name, I would will myself to Do Something Physical to show my surprise, appreciation, and excitement.

He did. I did. The audience cheered. It wasn't a whoop I gave, and it wasn't the Miss America tears that all good winners are supposed to deliver at a moment like that, but I'm convinced my full-body arm flap and the gasp I squeaked out did something to neutralize my Bake-Off freeze-up (if anybody's keeping track of such things). Also, in anticipation of the question about where the money would go, I had a ready answer: an iPod. Of course, an iPod doesn't make much of a dent in a $10,000 check, but I've decided it's fair for people to get some kind of answer to the inevitable question, instead of a polite side step.

In the spring of 2005 I submitted entries for the Rice to the Rescue recipe contest, sponsored by the United States Rice Federation, again following in Gadsby (and other big-name) footsteps. I didn't win the top prize of $5,000, but my Pear and Blue Cheese Salad was not entirely overlooked. The rice growers sent me a $1,000 check and a rice cooker that could vie for position on NASA's launch pad.

WHEN I won the Bake-Off, Carl and I were living in a nice house in a nice neighborhood with a nice-enough kitchen. There came a point, however, when I began to wonder why I didn't have a trophy kitchen. If I'm such a successful cook, I wondered, why don't I have a Sub-Zero fridge?

Meanwhile, we were contemplating a major move. Carl and I had lived in the Seattle area for all of our married life. With both of us now working at home, we didn't have to be located in the center of a big city. Any contact Carl needs to make with his clients is either by phone, e-mail, or site visit. We could live anywhere within range of our daughter, our granddaughter, and an international airport.

We settled on a small community on the Olympic Peninsula that's an hour's drive and a ferry ride out of Seattle. Though not intending to get involved in yet another remodel, we bought a house with a great location and a dumpy kitchen. Right away we began plans for upgrades.

I still had the image of a show-off kitchen, but when I went shopping for appliances and saw Sub-Zero's description, "An all stainless steel monument to food preservation," I knew I wouldn't be able to follow through. Even with the funds available, there are some things I cannot bring myself to do. I don't need to keep my eggs in an appliance built by hand. I only need something that will keep them cold.

The kitchen we ended up with is big enough to prepare and plate a four-course meal for eight, but modestly outfitted. I had a brief romance with the idea of a six-burner cooktop until I realized I couldn't remember a time I'd ever had four burners on all at once. We bought Ikea cabinets without fronts. Carl fashioned doors and drawers out of recycled wood, and they're gorgeous. The two of us working together cast concrete countertops. As the project's art director, I worked a ribbon of recycled glass chips into the polished tops. If other people's praise is any proof of our success, the results are good. Our work was featured on a recent community kitchen tour.

The group sponsoring the tour included a reference to my Pillsbury and Sutter Home wins as part of the promotion for their fund-raising event. A few of the 327 people who trooped through our kitchen that rainy Saturday had questions about my experience with the Bake-Off and cook-offs in general.

For what I hope are obvious reasons, I always encourage anyone who shows the slightest interest in competitive cooking. I'm living proof that success is not dependent on brilliance or great culinary skills.

I'm continually amazed by the number of people who deflect my encouragement. Their immediate excuses have become familiar to me. I heard them again the day of our kitchen tour. "I never measure anything." "I never make anything the same way twice." "I can never follow a recipe." "I've always been a lousy cook."

But consider the first time someone stirred a packet of dried onion soup into a carton of sour cream and called the results California Dip. Or the person who first tossed pretzels and nuts with a heap of breakfast cereal, and seasoned the mix with garlic and Worcestershire sauce to invent the snack we now call Nuts 'n' Bolts. Or the first person to slosh a little cocktail sauce over a brick of cream cheese, scatter a few baby shrimp over all, and serve with a dish of crackers as an appetizer. For that matter, someone somewhere was once the first person to slather peanut butter on one slice of bread, jelly on another, and put the two together.

Call it desperation. Call it invention. Call it a good idea. Any one of us is capable of finding something new under the sun. I meet people all the time who say, "Gee. I didn't know real people ever won those things." I'm here to tell you we do.

Salsa Couscous Chicken

PREP TIME: 30 MINUTES

START TO FINISH: 30 MINUTES

1 cup uncooked couscous or rice
Water
1 tablespoon olive or vegetable oil
¼ cup coarsely chopped almonds
2 cloves garlic, finely chopped
8 chicken thighs, skin removed
1 cup Old El Paso® Homestyle Garden Pepper or Thick 'n Chunky Salsa
¼ cup water
2 tablespoons dried currants or raisins
1 tablespoon honey
¾ teaspoon ground cumin
½ teaspoon ground cinnamon

1. Cook couscous in water as directed on package. Cover to keep warm.

2. Meanwhile, in 10-inch skillet, heat oil over medium-high heat until hot. Cook almonds in oil 1 to 2 minutes, stirring frequently, until golden brown. With slotted spoon, remove almonds from skillet; set aside.

3. Add garlic to skillet; cook and stir 30 seconds. Add chicken; cook 4 to 5 minutes or until browned, turning once.

4. In medium bowl, mix remaining ingredients. Add to chicken; mix well. Reduce heat to medium; cover and cook about 20 minutes, stirring occasionally, until chicken is fork-tender and juices run clear. Stir in almonds. Serve chicken mixture with couscous.

4 servings

High Altitude (3500–6500 ft): No change.

1 Serving: Calories 510 (Calories from Fat 170); Total Fat 19g (Saturated Fat 4.5g, Trans Fat 0g); Cholesterol 85mg; Sodium 470mg; Total Carbohydrate 48g (Dietary Fiber 4g, Sugars 11g); Protein 37g ■ **% Daily Value:** Vitamin A 6%; Vitamin C 0%; Calcium 10%; Iron 25% ■ **Exchanges:** 2 Starch, 1 Other Carbohydrate, 4½ Lean Meat, 1 Fat ■ **Carbohydrate Choices:** 3

Contest Name: Bake-Off® Contest 38, 1998
Contestant Name: Ellie Mathews
City: Seattle
State: WA
Prize Value: $1,000,000 Grand Prize Winner